BETTER
BEHAVIOUR

Sara Miller McCune founded SAGE Publishing in 1965 to support the dissemination of usable knowledge and educate a global community. SAGE publishes more than 1000 journals and over 800 new books each year, spanning a wide range of subject areas. Our growing selection of library products includes archives, data, case studies and video. SAGE remains majority owned by our founder and after her lifetime will become owned by a charitable trust that secures the company's continued independence.

Los Angeles | London | New Delhi | Singapore | Washington DC | Melbourne

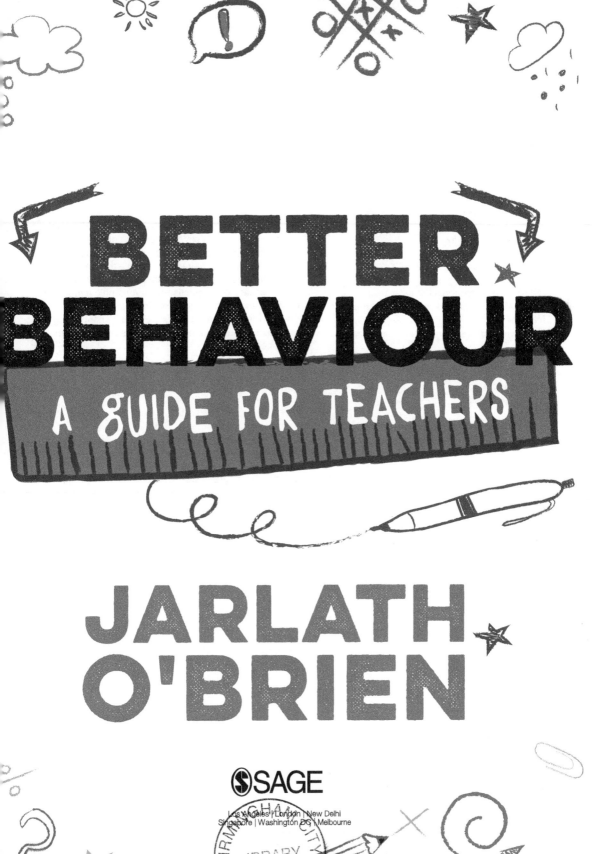

BETTER BEHAVIOUR

A GUIDE FOR TEACHERS

JARLATH O'BRIEN

SAGE

Los Angeles | London | New Delhi
Singapore | Washington DC | Melbourne

Los Angeles | London | New Delhi
Singapore | Washington DC | Melbourne

SAGE Publications Ltd
1 Oliver's Yard
55 City Road
London EC1Y 1SP

SAGE Publications Inc.
2455 Teller Road
Thousand Oaks, California 91320

SAGE Publications India Pvt Ltd
B 1/I 1 Mohan Cooperative Industrial Area
Mathura Road
New Delhi 110 044

SAGE Publications Asia-Pacific Pte Ltd
3 Church Street
#10-04 Samsung Hub
Singapore 049483

Editor: James Clark
Editorial assistant: Diana Alves
Production editor: Thea Watson
Copyeditor: Elaine Leek
Indexer: Anne Solamito
Marketing manager: Dilhara Attygalle
Cover design: Naomi Robinson
Typeset by: C&M Digitals (P) Ltd, Chennai, India
Printed in the UK

© Jarlath O'Brien 2018

First published 2018

Library of Congress Control Number: 2017958867

British Library Cataloguing in Publication data

A catalogue record for this book is available from the British Library

ISBN 978-1-5264-2972-8
ISBN 978-1-5264-2973-5 (pbk)

At SAGE we take sustainability seriously. Most of our products are printed in the UK using responsibly sourced papers and boards. When we print overseas we ensure sustainable papers are used as measured by the PREPS grading system. We undertake an annual audit to monitor our sustainability.

A little child is only heart; he thrives off relationships; his joy is in relationships; he grows through relationships. When he is in communion with someone he trusts, he is safe, he is someone, someone unique and important.

Jean Vanier, *Becoming Human*

CONTENTS

ABOUT THE AUTHOR

 Jarlath has been a teacher for nearly two decades. He has worked in comprehensive, independent, selective and special education, including in schools for children with social, emotional and behavioural difficulties, and severe and profound and multiple learning difficulties. For the last seven years Jarlath has been a Headteacher and Executive Headteacher.

Jarlath is the behaviour columnist for *TES*, has written for *The Guardian* and for several other education publications and trains teachers on behaviour, school leadership and special educational needs.

ACKNOWLEDGEMENTS

Emma for putting up with an absent husband who was writing when I should have been spending time with her.

Hannah for keeping me grounded – 'You're not even the first dad in my class to write a book. Olivia's dad wrote one ages ago, and he gave a copy to Mrs Forrester.'

Aidan for riding with me on those long runs in the woods that helped to pull all my thoughts together.

Sue Urwin, Stewart Tait, Kola Odeniyi, Andy Dalgleish, Brent Woodley, Garry Bowler, Elsie Nyamapfene and Carol Goodridge from Millside School, and Nathan Aspinall, Pat Pringle, Kathleen Brown, Katie Axford, Sonia Kay, Val Barlow and Annette Meier from Holyport Manor School who all taught me so much and who showed just what is possible when a team pulls together in even the most challenging of circumstances.

Tom Vodden, whose training on behaviour was the best part of my teacher training and who continues to make me think deeply about behaviour. And for the biscuits.

Jon Severs who provided me with my first opportunities to write about behaviour and who taught me to tighten up my thinking and writing on this topic.

Damian Milton for his advice and guidance on autism and sensory issues.

Mark Finnis for offering his views on restorative approaches to resolving conflict.

Claire Ryan for offering the parent's point of view.

James Clark, Rob Patterson and Diana Alves at SAGE for asking me to write this book and for their professional assistance in making the idea a reality.

INTRODUCTION

There comes a point where we need to stop just pulling people out of the river. We need to go upstream and find out why they're falling in.

Archbishop Desmond Tutu

I didn't always think the way I do now about the behaviour of children in schools

I have been a teacher for 17 years, starting my teaching life in a comprehensive school in Wokingham teaching science and then working successively in a selective boys independent school, a special school for children with social, emotional and behavioural difficulties (SEBD), a large special school for children with severe (SLD) and profound and multiple learning difficulties (PMLD) and autism, a special school for children with moderate learning difficulties (MLD), and now for a family of special schools. I have worked with children from the age of 2 to young adults of 19. I have worked with children who have gone to Oxford or Cambridge and children who have gone to prison. I have worked with children who have died due to life-shortening conditions. This breadth and depth has given me an invaluable perspective on children's behaviour in schools and on how to improve it.

My thinking and, more importantly, my actions, my feelings and my attitude have evolved significantly in that time such that the person and teacher I am now bears as much comparison with the person and newly qualified teacher I was in 2001 as a human does with its early modern human ancestor; recognisably similar in both form and shape, but fundamentally different in terms of maturity, skills and sophistication. I use the word 'evolved' deliberately. Everything about me and my actions has changed gradually over time – a direct consequence of having to adapt to the different schools and situations I found myself in or because of the many mistakes I have made. These were the evolutionary pressures, if I am to stretch this analogy, which caused, and sometimes forced me to reflect and commit to changing my practice. I made mistakes. A lot. But I learned from them.

In my first week as a newly-qualified teacher (NQT) in 2001 – 11 September 2001, to be precise, the day of the terrorist attack on the World Trade Center in Manhattan – I stood in the teachers' professional development centre in Wokingham as all NQTs were welcomed to the borough by a number of local authority officers and councillors.

'Welcome to Wokingham,' one councillor beamed. 'You've come to the right place. We don't have any badly behaved children in this borough,' she boasted.

'Interesting,' I said, to Zoe, a fellow NQT next to me. 'I was told to fuck off 2 hours ago by a kid in Year 10.'

I didn't set out to think this way. I am 6 feet tall with a big voice and initially when I began working in a comprehensive school I naïvely thought that my 'presence' in the classroom (that elusive term we use to describe teachers who seem to ooze effortless authority, the ones who appear to silence a room with an imperceptible raising of their eyebrow) was enough for most children to get the message that I was the boss in that room. The word 'presence' reminds me of our PGCE course director when he told us of his memorable first lesson teaching a notorious class history in a secondary modern in the 1970s. He walked into the room and threw his leather satchel towards his desk from the other side of the room so the noise when it landed would make an emphatic thud signifying his arrival. He missed and the bag flew straight through the plate glass window next to his desk and out on to the ground, one floor below. Without pausing for breath he cracked on with the lesson to stunned silence, the children thinking he'd done it on purpose.

I didn't have to think deeply about behaviour with the majority of children with whom I worked, and I don't think the schools I worked in thought deeply about behaviour either. Whatever I wanted the students to do, they did for the most part. I seemed to have a knack of getting on with most of the children deemed unteachable by some ('Anyone working below GCSE Grade C, Jarlath, is unteachable. Fact.'), but I never considered why. The rest were, as far as I was concerned, choosing (a word I am likely to come back to a number of times in this book) to misbehave. I held the view, one I am concerned is now becoming more widespread, that any and all deviations from my expectations were simply premeditated choices to be naughty. The solutions, or so I thought, were simple too. Deviations were to be countered with punishment until the miscreants learned the errors of their ways. Bill Rogers describes the use of the word punishment as absurd – 'We're not running a prison'. It was, and remains, a seductive state of mind that places all of the reasons for behavioural difficulties and all of the responsibility for changing with the child. The school and teachers simply set out their policy and rules and the children have to fit in. I was wrong. I worked in schools where silence, compliance and control (not undesirable in and of themselves when required for obvious reasons, but poor proxies for learning) were considered the immediate indicators of highly effective teaching and, by extension I presume, learning but we never went that far in our discussions. In fact, I'll go further – the teachers who scared the children, and there were a handful that prided themselves on this, were considered the best teachers in the school. That's how deeply we seemed to think about the behaviour of children. I went along with it in the early days in a sort of 'monkey see, monkey do' fashion, but the knot of uneasiness in my belly grew ever larger. The children who would behave well under any system that we devised behaved well and many of the others who struggled under such a system just ricocheted from ineffective punishment to ineffective punishment in a never-ending cycle of failure or they disappeared after a while and we never saw them again. This was not a system that improved behaviour; it just moved the behaviour, and the child along with it, somewhere else.

The kind of empty, and frankly unhelpful, advice that I was offered is, I fear, trotted out in schools on a daily basis, and has been for generations, but does nothing to improve our understanding or our effectiveness. Unhelpful because these tactics are often plucked off the shelf without a thought as to the climate in the classroom and the relationships underpinning everything that goes on in there:

'Put them in a boy/girl alphabetical seating plan.'

'Kids crave boundaries.'

'They're just doing it for attention.'

'Get them to devise their own set of class rules and they'll stick to them because they own them.'

'They're just choosing to be naughty.'

I fear that there is nothing underpinning these neat one-liners and they leave teachers who genuinely seek support and deeper understanding no further forward. To be clear, I am not necessarily against some of these things. A seating plan may well be a smart move, but I would encourage you to give its layout more consideration than simply by gender and their place in the register (more on this in Chapter 4). I presume that the rationale behind the above plan is that it removes all trace of agency from the children and that, given the choice, they would opt to sit with their friends (probable) and therefore disruption will inevitably follow (not necessarily). I was always happy to give my classes the responsibility to choose where to sit and to show that they could work well under such an arrangement. But, I was always explicit with them all that I reserved the right to seat students where I wanted without notice. Did I ever have to move children? Yes, but it was an occasional thing. Do kids need boundaries? Of course they do, but I don't think they crave them explicitly. They need to feel safe and secure in your classroom and in your company and boundaries are one vital part of providing that. Feeling safe and secure in your classroom and in your company goes way, way beyond the presence of boundaries. Your boundaries could be prohibitively restrictive, too loose or, far worse, porous, all of which will lead to an uneasiness amongst the students. On my first full day as a Headteacher I was on playground duty at break time when a TA nervously sidled up to me and asked me 'What do you think about running in the playground?' 'Er ... I would encourage it,' I responded, thinking it was a trick question. It wasn't; the rule, up until that minute, was that there could be no running in the playground.

I have lost count of the times I have heard, 'they're just doing it for attention' and seen teachers left hanging thinking 'does that mean I give it to them or deny them the attention?' The discussion seldom seems to move on to ascertaining the purpose of the attention. Whenever I hear 'they're just doing it for attention' I find it helpful to replace that with the question 'Why is this child seeking some control over this situation?' In this book I'll seek to provide you with the depth I wish I had in the first decade of my teaching life so that you're not left wondering if the grizzled veteran in the staffroom is joking when he says, 'whatever you do, do not smile at the kids until Christmas'. I'll save you the bother. Smile. Smile lots. At everyone.

At intervals throughout that gradual evolution there were specific incidents in my teaching life that caused an irreversible step-change (a punctuated evolution if you will) in my thinking, actions, feelings and attitude. We have all had them, some fleeting and incidental, others traumatic and profound. Times such as:

Stephen running across the car park and punching me in the head

This happened days after I had completed a week's course to become a tutor in restrictive physical intervention. I stood in the school car park, rooted to the spot, laptop in one hand, lever-arch file in the other, as Stephen ran from one end of the car park to the other screaming that he was going to hit me. Despite my training, and, to his credit, his clear warning complete with expletives for added emphasis, I did nothing. I stood there honestly believing that nothing would happen. He then proceeded to punch me in the head. At least I didn't drop the laptop.

Michael trying to get in to my science laboratory by using a scaffold pole as a battering ram

Michael was relatively new to our school and had smashed the driver's side window of our minibus on his first day in our school. Being a positive person I took great heart from the fact that he was trying to get *in* to my lesson.

Sophie deliberately and repeatedly hitting her head on the side of the swimming pool

Sophie did this despite the obvious pain in order to see the patterns and swirls the drops of blood made in the water and she seemed to enjoy the metallic taste it made in her mouth. Sophie also did this on concrete or on mirrors too.

Richard looking me straight in the eye and saying, 'You don't understand me at all do you?'

Richard had joined our special school from a mainstream secondary school and it is fair to say that it took me longer than I would normally expect to figure out a plan of action for Richard to feel safe and successful in our school. He could see right through me and told me straight to my face. I still thank him for it.

Dylan's mum spending *4 months* in lessons with him, her adopted son, before they were both prepared to separate from each other

Would you have a parent in your class for 4 months? That's what it took for Dylan, and his mum, to feel safe and be prepared to separate so that's what we had to do to support them.

Seanie responding to each request to write with 'I can't write; I've got a bad hand.'

I know now, but failed to spot at the time, that Seanie was avoiding revealing to everyone present that his writing skills, and reading whilst we're at it, were not as good as he would have liked.

You cannot come out the other side of situations such as these unchanged. Managing these situations successfully and understanding the context in which they occurred left me with an inner confidence that I could handle much of what any school day could throw at me and, equally importantly, support colleagues through the same. Crucially I thought deeply about how to create the conditions to prevent, as far as is possible, these things recurring or happening in the first place.

We all have a number of these memorable experiences that have shaped us and shifted our practice, the lessons and feelings of which never leave us. My wife, Emma, is fond of telling of the time as an NQT teaching Years 5 and 6 when a group of boys came in first thing in the morning announcing with jubilation, 'Miss King! Harry's waving a dildo around in the cloakroom!'

Mentally flicking through her teacher training manual and coming up with a blank page, Emma warily ventured into the cloakroom.

'Where did you get that from, Harry?'

'I found it in a skip on the way to school, Miss.'

Deciding that getting the thing out of sight as soon as possible was the swiftest way to defuse this situation, she fetched a bin, persuading Harry to part company with it before washing his hands and giving him a job to do to keep him busy.

'At least it didn't belong to his mum,' she says.

There is, though, one particular situation that changed me as a person and a teacher more than any other with regard to behaviour. I had been struggling to build a working relationship with one girl in Year 10 and this was beginning to affect the entire class. After one particularly difficult lesson I went to a senior leader, considered to be the behaviour guru in school, asking for help and advice. I admitted to having significant difficulties, which made me feel very vulnerable, and was sad to be met with the response, 'Read this.' A pamphlet by educational psychologist Rob Long (for whom I have a great deal of respect, by the way) was chucked my way and it was clear that the conversation was over. No offers of a follow-up, no drop-ins, no mentoring, no listening. Maybe they were under significant pressure or they felt I was moaning unnecessarily, but I left that office determined, in the absence of support from above, to take personal responsibility for my own development, think more, learn more and improve. It is also a lesson I have never forgotten now that I am a Headteacher too.

Looking back, that incident was probably the real beginning of my journey on this road to understanding behaviour in as much depth and with as much empathy as I could, and of improving it. It started with me as a class teacher trying to improve things in my own science laboratory and eventually moved on to me becoming a Headteacher trying to improve things across an entire school. In my early days as a Headteacher it is true that I struggled to get a critical mass of my colleagues to believe that my principles were going to be effective and this lack of consistency from adults showed in the behaviour of some of the children we worked with. However, it took just 15 months for the judgement of England's schools' inspectorate, Ofsted, on the behaviour of our children to move from Requires Improvement to Outstanding (their top grade). Incidentally this was done without the use of exclusion – a school does not improve behaviour by getting rid of a swathe of its population, it just changes the cohort. Our confidence as a group of professionals grew as we embraced the ways of thinking, acting and speaking that I will discuss in detail in the following chapters and this too showed in the behaviour of the children we worked with. The confidence grew because we could draw on the knowledge that we had tackled similar situations before with a successful outcome for the children and the adults. In short, we knew we could do it.

This book is entitled *Better Behaviour* because any book offering advice to teachers on this most important of topics must lead to improvements in the behaviour of children (it will change your behaviour too, by the way, and that is, ultimately, the real point of this book). If it doesn't achieve this aim of improving behaviour then this book is simply a solution to a wobbly table. But be under no illusions, significant behaviour change takes time, in the same way that losing weight and keeping it off takes time. This book could also equally be called *Feeling Better About Behaviour* as it will change your emotions on this most emotive of topics. Do not underestimate this aspect of improving the behaviour of children. Our own emotions are extremely powerful and we significantly underestimate quite how much they can influence both our own decision-making and the behaviours of others at our peril – my time as a Special Constable with Thames Valley Police taught me this and a whole lot more about the behaviour of human beings too. This book will only achieve both of these twin aims if you too, like me, commit to changing the things you do, the way you think and the words you use. As Paul Dix says, 'When the adults change, everything changes.' He's right.

'Is teaching an art or a science?' is a question I often hear posed. For me it is a craft, and understanding and improving the behaviour of children is a fundamental part of that craft. It requires skills and knowledge that need to be honed, developed and shaped over time and that can only truly be achieved by a constant cycle of practice and reflection.

And so, after nearly two decades of constant practice and reflection I know the following to be true:

- Some children regard schools as risky, unsafe places to be, where failure is inevitable and painful and must be avoided at all costs.

- Lasting behaviour change takes time.

- Learning needs to be an intrinsically rewarding experience.

- Negative behaviour communicates an unmet need.

- Behavioural difficulties can be regarded as demonstrations of skills gaps that are getting in the way of a child being successful.

- Sometimes we choose actions, sanctions and punishments that only meet the needs of adults. We do this in order to say that we dealt with a situation but, in reality, the situation remains, at best, unchanged. At worst, damaged.

- Time invested in children is never wasted.

I'll expand on these in the coming chapters. I hope that this book will challenge your thinking, broaden your repertoire of skills, improve your confidence and reduce your frustrations about improving the behaviour of the children with whom you work. Lofty aims, but ones I'm sure you'll agree are worth it for all concerned.

Good luck!

1

WHY UNDERSTANDING BEHAVIOUR MATTERS

As soon as we start selecting and judging people instead of welcoming them as they are – with their sometimes hidden beauty, as well as their more frequently visible weakness – we are reducing life, not fostering it.

Jean Vanier

THE HEADLINES

- If you aren't in control in your classroom, then someone else will be.
- Understanding behaviour means you are better equipped to:
  o manage situations in your classroom;
  o support children when they need you the most;
  o support other colleagues;
  o plan for success;
  o reduce your own stress;
  o build strong relationships with parents.
- Think about children's behavioural development with the same attention to detail that you give their academic progress.
- Take account of the differences in a child's physical, emotional and cognitive development.
- Teach children explicitly the language and behaviour of conflict resolution. Teach the differences between statements, promises and responsibilities.
- Be sensitive as to where and how feedback is given.
- Never use shame.
- Develop a culture where mistakes are used to push on everyone's understanding.
- Understand that work avoidance can be an effective way to sidestep failure.
- Aim for independence. They've got to be able to manage when you're not there any more.

It is self-evident why behaviour matters. If a child or children in your class are not behaving the way you need them to then they will be unable to take part in your lesson in the way you planned and to learn as well as you would like. In addition there is the risk that the learning of other students is disrupted and this is unacceptable for obvious reasons. Sound simple? On one level, yes, it is simple, but for me this issue is a much broader and far deeper one. I worry that a proportion of the profession have not taken their thinking beyond this and are, as a result, perennially frustrated. That is why *understanding* behaviour matters. A lack of understanding can leave a teacher feeling powerless and there is nothing worse for a teacher than feeling that things are out of their control. *If you aren't in control in your classroom, then who is?*

Understanding what is going on behind the behaviour is important for a number of reasons:

- It means you are equipped with the knowledge and understanding to manage situations and improve the behaviour of children.
- You feel more confident to manage situations that may be unfamiliar to you. This confidence will manifest itself in that 'presence' mentioned earlier.
- You are more likely to plan for success in advance, knowing likely triggers and stressors.
- You are better prepared to support the child or children at precisely the time when they need you the most, including the other children around the situation.
- You are better able to support colleagues in the heat of the moment or in a planned, coaching way.
- The stress that you may experience is likely to be lower as you retain a stronger sense of control.
- You build trust with parents as they are reassured that you haven't written their child off as the naughty one and are seeking understanding in order to improve the child's behaviour.

Coping with the demands of the school environment and emotional self-regulation

Toddlers are inherently egocentric and selfish and parents make great efforts to teach them to share possessions with others, learn to wait and to follow many other social norms as they are prone to want whatever they desire instantly. We are especially keen for these habits of emotional self-regulation to be firmly in place by the time that young children start school, but the reality of life means that children start school at different levels of emotional development and some are less emotionally mature than others.

We need to stop describing children as school-ready and start describing schools as child-ready

Biesta (2015[1]) describes this as the medicalisation of education, 'where children are being made fit for the educational system, rather than that we ask where the causes of this misfit lie and who, therefore, needs treatment most: the child or society.'

The structures, rules and expectations of schools and the presence of many more children than they are probably used to place demands on these young children and some can find the transition from a home, childminder and/or nursery environment difficult to handle. There is a similar level of challenge when children move from primary school to secondary school. The rules and expectations may be broadly the same but the physical size of the school, the number of students there, the number of teachers the children have and the amount of homework, to name but a few factors, are all vastly greater. Coping with all these changes places great demands on 11-year-olds and this is why schools invest time in transition. It is no coincidence that a number of children join our special school each year from mainstream secondary schools because they struggle with the social and organisational demands placed upon them. Ostensibly their placement has broken down because of their behaviour, but there is often an underlying learning and/or communication difficulty that has not been met well enough to enable the child to feel successful (how you define 'successful' for a child in a school is, of course, open to debate).

Early years professionals are very good at working out what stage children are at in their emotional development and at building the skills of children over time. Well, almost all of them. A friend of mine, herself a very skilled behaviour expert, enjoys telling of the time she and her husband were called to their daughter's nursery where the manager informed them their daughter was to be put on a behaviour plan as she was biting other children. The child in question was 12 months old. I hope this little toddler understood the seriousness of the situation and sorted herself out.

It should come as no surprise, therefore, that one of the core components of the Early Years Foundation Stage profile (the assessment framework for children before Year 1) is called Personal, Social and Emotional Development (split up into three areas: self-confidence and self-awareness; managing feelings and behaviour; making relationships).

I contend that teachers are generally less prone to think about the gaps in the emotional development of children the older the children get. With hindsight, I can see that thinking in this formative way about the behaviour of children, the way I and every other teacher in the land think about the academic work those same children are doing, would have helped me in my first few years as a teacher in a comprehensive school. It is certainly true that becoming a parent helped with this. Prior to that I had little to do with children below the age of 11 and had precisely no knowledge of child development (a major gap in my PGCE teacher training). Watching my own children grow from helpless newborns to speaking and then reading their first words and understanding all of the steps that had to be in place for that to happen filled in a lot of the gaps for me. It also helped me appreciate the problems that can surface when some of those steps are missing. I will never forget working with Dylan (mentioned in the Introduction). He had been abused as a baby and been adopted after a period of time in foster care. He can have no conscious memory of what happened to him as a baby, yet that abuse manifested itself in his behaviour every single day 15 years later.

Looking for and understanding the gaps in the development of children is a skill that teachers in special schools would regard as second nature. They are used to their children having, as they would describe it, a 'spiky profile'. That is to say the children are at different stages of maturity in their cognitive, emotional and social and physical development and they factor this into much of what they do. I've worked with teenagers going through puberty, who may be working at the cognitive level of a 10-year-old and with the emotional maturity of a 5-year-old, for example. Failure to take these differences into account would be doing a disservice to that child.

REFLECTION POINTS

What is the quality of the information held in your school on the social and emotional development of your children?

Have a think about some of the children you're working with. I'll bet you could tell me the ins and outs of their academic progress in fine detail. Your school probably has spreadsheets, progress grids, tracker sheets, all neatly colour-coded to prove how well the children are doing academically. Think of the hours you spend feeding information into that machine. Now think about the depth of knowledge held in the school on the social, emotional and behavioural development of the children. There's probably no comparison. Almost all of what is known will be held separately in the heads of the staff working with those children. Many subjects are split into strands – reading, writing and speaking and listening in English, for example – yet when we think of behaviour it could just be as blunt as 'Good or Naughty'.

Tools such as the Boxall Profile[2] or Fagus[3] can really help to fill any knowledge gaps in your school on the social and emotional development of the children you're all working with, set developmentally appropriate targets and then monitor how the children are getting on against those targets. Fagus, for example, divides social and emotional development into 13 domains:

---

cognitive development, language development, attachment, self-concept, motivation and self-efficacy, self-esteem, self-control, awareness and understanding of others, socialisation, moral development, play, coping and self-awareness. There is a richness in there with a psychological underpinning that allows you to move beyond thinking (labelling, in reality – see Chapter 2 on faulty thinking) of children as good or naughty.

Whilst a checklist or profiling tool doesn't improve behaviour by itself, it will shorten the time you spend action planning, focus your efforts and it does allow you to deepen collective knowledge and use a common language with your colleagues – and the parents too don't forget – about the emotional development of the children with whom you are working. Crucially too it will help you celebrate progress and successes with the child along the way. It is far harder to do this when children are labelled good or naughty, for when does a child move from the good list to the naughty list? Let's leave that decision to Father Christmas. If you think that no teacher or school would do such a thing then consider the widespread use of names on the board for misdemeanours, or traffic light charts (see Chapter 6 for more on this).

- What will you now do differently?

- How can you improve on the quality of information held?

- What will you do with it?

- Who will you share it with?

Time spent in schools is an intensely social experience and so you can see that it is vital that all children we work with are able to manage the significant social demands each school day places on them. They also need to be able to manage the rigid nature of the school timetable. When the timetable says it is English, it is English, whether the child likes it or not or, more likely, when the timetable says it is Mr O'Brien, it is Mr O'Brien (or Mr No'Brain as I was once brilliantly called), whether the child likes it or not. Primary teachers can have more flexibility and can extend an activity or lesson that is working very well and that they are loath to stop or, equally usefully, they can cut short a lesson that is dying on its feet (we've all been there). I had no such luxury as a secondary school physics teacher. When the bell went, off they trooped to the next lesson on their timetable. Many times some of the children I taught would have loved an extra 20 minutes with me as they were either engrossed in black holes, magnetism or somesuch and they felt they were doing really well or they wanted to delay going to their next lesson. Equally, there will have been many times when some of the children I taught couldn't wait for the lesson with me to finish, either because of my lesson itself or because they couldn't wait to get to their next lesson.

Either way, they had to manage the disappointment or elation of leaving my classroom and head off to their next lesson with a sense of anticipation, dread or indifference.

REFLECTION POINTS

How do you prepare children for changes, both expected and unexpected, during the school day?

Teachers in special schools spend significant amounts of time working on transitions. Not just moving from lesson to lesson, but often managing the changes between activities in a lesson – moving from the story on the carpet to written work on the group tables in an infant class, for example, or from a science experiment to analysing the data on a computer in secondary. They extend this to preparing children for changes such as the absence of the expected teacher due to illness or at times of the year such as Christmas or late July when large parts of the established routine can be changed temporarily. Are there children that you work with who would benefit from some preparation for changes within lessons and between lessons or for unexpected changes such as staff absence? There are many ways to do this, but failing to do it will simply result in some children filling the void with concern or anxiety which makes things harder for all of you. For some children a conversation is all it takes. They are simply made aware of what is coming up that is different and that is enough. For others it might take the form of a *First–Next–Last* visual strip on their desk. First – English (Miss Hardy), Next – Break time (playground), Last – PE (Mrs Ormerod). A colleague of mine is the form tutor of a class of children in a special school, all of whom have autism. Their morning routine in registration involves the construction of their colour-coded timetable each day comprising the lesson, the teacher and the location on Velcro strips. Changes such as staff illness are communicated each morning in this way and the children carry these timetables around with them all day, depositing each lesson in a specially prepared box as they arrive at each classroom. The level of detail required quite clearly depends on the needs of each child, but the basic structure is the same.

- What will you now do differently?

Lastly, you won't be surprised to learn there is research that shows that self-regulation has a stronger correlation with school readiness (the researchers' words, not mine) than IQ or entry-level reading or maths skills,[4] can lead to higher academic achievement[5] and that teachers can have a positive effect on children's self-regulation skills.[6] Professor Linda J. Graham from the Faculty of Education at Queensland University of Technology (QUT) has conducted recent research, commenting that 'we're finding that children's ability to self-regulate has a large bearing on educational outcomes and that self-regulation is affected by many things, including age and gender. Unfortunately, this sets some kids up for conflict with their teachers, some of whom find it difficult to understand why some of the children in their class find it difficult to control their bodies and emotions, whilst other children seem not to have any problem at all.'[7]

Managing conflict and disagreement

That ability to regulate one's own emotions in order to cope with the demands of school is clearly vital, but it is a skill that has wider benefits. Children falling out with each other at school is as predictable as a downpour on a bank holiday weekend, but we expect children to move on from the toddler-type reaction of hitting another child over the head with the plastic toy that the other child is trying to take from them or, as in the case above, biting the other child to make them let go. Teachers all over the world spend precious time supporting children to resolve conflicts with each other; this is time that could, if freed up by their ability to manage conflict and disagreement on their own or, more preferably, avoid it happening in the first place, be put to good use tackling the lengthy to-do lists that we all have.

Children who manage relationships well and deal with conflict and disagreement in a mature way are, I contend, more likely to grow up to be adults who manage relationships well and deal with conflict and disagreement in a mature way. I saw the other, ugly side of this when I worked for Thames Valley Police. A significant amount of my time as a Special Constable was spent dealing with conflict and disagreement between adults, including domestic violence, that had escalated to violence against other people (or themselves) or property, sometimes fuelled by alcohol or other drugs. The financial cost to the state, and the costs, financial, emotional and otherwise to them, their victims and the families involved on either side, were significant. Getting things right as early as possible is the best preventative work available. There will be more on the use of restorative practices in Chapter 7.

Explicit teaching of the language of resolution and what resolution actually looks like pays off with children. Mark Finnis, a restorative practices trainer, makes a big deal of the fact that there is a big difference between empty statements and gestures, promises and responsibilities.

Statements such as 'I'm really sorry for hitting you' can indeed be heartfelt and sincere, but they carry with them no commitment to behave differently in the future. Sorry is a word we hear time and again in schools, but it can be a throwaway remark; it can be cheap. For many children (and adults, if we're honest) it is the learned response to a situation that marks in their mind that they've apologised, and that is all that is required to make the situation better; mentally they move on without giving the situation or people caught up in it another thought. It is a learned response because adults have led them to understand that this is the way problems are resolved. 'Say sorry,' and, as far as the child can see, that is the end of the matter. 'Say it like you mean it!' may well follow if the teacher is not satisfied that enough remorse has been demonstrated. This can unhelpfully escalate a situation and, as Bill Rogers says 'It's tempting to want to confront, even embarrass, students in order to "win" – but win what?'[8] Promises such as 'This won't happen again' certainly do contain a commitment to behave differently in the future and you can see how children can be held to account for those promises at a later time if problems do reoccur. Questions such as 'How can I fix our friendship?' are where the real power lies. Imagine the kinds of discussions you can support (and you undoubtedly do need to support these kinds of discussions, especially with younger children, for them to become meaningful) when the children talk in this way. There will be more detail in Chapter 7 on this, including scripts to help you get started.

I had one such conversation with two teenagers who came to blows in a football match one break time. One of the two boys was desperate to get the meeting over with and kept repeating 'sorry, sorry, I'm really sorry'. Interestingly he was saying this to me and not the other boy. He struggled when I asked him to explain why he was sorry and what he was actually sorry for. The discussion needed to be managed by me for it to be meaningful, but getting to the point where both were able to talk about their responsibilities towards each other in the future took time. But it was time well spent.

Interestingly one week after I'd written the paragraph above I was asked to talk to two more boys, both 13 and with learning difficulties, about a falling out they'd had during a different football match (yes, yes, I know. I need to look at what's happening on the astroturf at break and lunchtimes). When I approached them in the playground I said that I needed to get them together and before I could even finish my sentence Faisal said to me, 'Don't worry about it, sir. We've sorted it out between ourselves.' 'Are you happy with that, Eddie?' I asked of the other child. 'Yep, all done,' he replied and off they went. Ideally they wouldn't have fallen out in the first place, but resolving their difference themselves saved me time and means they are more likely to do so again in the future should further disagreements or conflict happen and, I hope, reduce the likelihood of such things actually reoccurring at all.

Reducing bullying

It follows that children who are emotionally secure, good at getting on with other people and good at resolving disagreement are less likely to bully others or be resistant to being bullied themselves. Every school experiences bullying, and resolving it swiftly is always a priority for teachers and school leaders. However, bullying can persist and this is problematic for all concerned. Parents can lose confidence if they feel a teacher's or school's strategies are ineffective as they rightly demand that their child be free from harm whilst in your care. Restorative practices are one of the most effective ways to reduce bullying and, ideally, prevent it rearing its ugly head later on. As with managing conflicts and disagreements above, I will cover restorative practices in Chapter 7.

This parental confidence was sorely tested when I first became a Headteacher. A mother and father, two of our school's strongest advocates, met with me repeatedly over the course of a couple of weeks as I grappled with a bullying problem that their son was coping with. I explained how we would resolve this using restorative means, but the mother said pointedly, 'Everything you're saying sounds very nice. Trouble is, I don't believe you. I don't believe this will actually work.' All I could weakly say in response was that they would judge me by how things panned out. The bullying stopped. Admittedly it took a little longer than I was content with, but it stopped. The father later told me that they were 'this close' (think of the smallest gap you can indicate with your fingers, halve it and then halve it again) to taking their son out of our school.

As a Headteacher I could have used fixed-term exclusion (suspending a child for one or more days from school) as a punishment and, knowing the parents of the victim well, this would have met with some immediate approval. I know, though, that the situation would have remained unresolved and the attitude of the bully unchanged. Yes, the bully may have spent a short period of time away from the school, thus ensuring that the victim was free from bullying for that time, but it would have done nothing to improve his behaviour. The thinking behind the idea that simply by being away from school for a period of time changes the behaviour of any child is superficial. It is sometimes portrayed as a 'short, sharp shock', the logic being that the child is stunned into improving their behaviour because they are upset or traumatised at the thought of being prevented from attending school. This logic – simply a question of the attitude of the child – is, at best, tenuous. As Patrick, 17 and a former student of ours (again, one who left a secondary school because of his behaviour), recently so neatly put it when we were discussing exclusion, 'Easy. Excluded means a lie-in and Xbox.' The point that usually follows, that exclusion is a deterrent and an example is set to others is, I am convinced, wishful thinking.

This approach can be a hard sell to some teachers as it can seem permissive or soft. I am obsessed with improving behaviour. I am not interested in grand gestures to show how tough I am as a teacher or school leader. If bullying reoccurs once the child is back in school then I have done nothing to support the children, staff or parents. It leads down a road to permanent exclusion which means the victim is no longer bullied by that child at school, but the other child is elsewhere, behaviour unchanged and with a deeper feeling of negativity and rejection about schools in general, potentially repeating the same behaviours towards another child. I will cover this in more detail in Chapter 6 on sanctions, punishments and consequences.

Coping with feedback and criticism

Have you ever been on the receiving end of some criticism of your work? It doesn't feel good does it? Clearly it matters how the message is delivered, but the bottom line is that, even with the gentlest delivery, someone else holds the view that your work and, by extension, you if you take it personally (which is hard not to do and I certainly have a tendency to do so), is not good enough. Not convinced? Tell your partner what you really think about their driving the next time you're in the car together. And don't say I didn't warn you.

> *Your thinking is pedestrian and you have no leadership skills whatsoever.*
>
> (Feedback on my application to the Fast Track school leadership programme, 2004.)

The heavy feeling in the pit of your belly, the same one I got (and can still feel) when the comment above was said to my face, can be magnified if you've put everything you've got into that piece of work and that feeling can be doubly strong if the person delivering the message is very important to us. The cocktail of emotions that can surface as a result needs to be managed somehow. As adults we may have significant flexibility in our working day so that we can cope with this by deciding to walk around the block in our free period or call our partner or a colleague for advice. Besides, if our boss has an ounce of humanity the discussion will have been in private anyway. It's not likely that the feedback from a lesson observation that we spent the night before fretting about would be delivered in a staff meeting in front of 30 of our colleagues. The children we work with, perhaps in full view of their peers, may have to simply sit there and take it on the chin. Clearly, for the majority of children receiving feedback is a part of school life that they are used to and accept. They cope with advice in the form of written marking and verbal feedback all the time and see it as positive. They accept that it is given with the best intentions and not used to shame them publicly because their relationship with the teacher is on solid ground and they use that feedback to improve their work, but this is not universal.

I still feel sad when I recall how Mrs Rogers publicly ridiculed my attempts to identify tenths, hundredths and thousandths when I was in Year 6:

'Which number is in the tenths column?'

'Three?' [tentatively]

'Wrong! Try again.'

'Eight?' [weakly]

'Wrong! Try again.'

I was resorting to guessing now. I blush easily so I must have been puce by this point.

'Nine?' [barely whispering]

'You don't have a clue! You could do with being like Elaine sat next to you.'

I didn't know what that meant then and I don't know even now. What's worse is that I had a thing for Elaine and felt sure that this public dressing down ruined my chances with her. Thirty-one years ago, but the legacy of that minute remains to this day.

My son's lovely school helpfully lay out all the children's exercise books on parents' evenings so we can leaf through them whilst we're waiting to see the teacher. It was clear that the school had a policy of getting the children to respond in written form to the teacher's marking. I noticed in my son's books, but not in my daughter's interestingly, that he had two stock responses to comments from the teacher. If the teacher's comments were in the form of praise (or, as he would say, positive) he would always write 'Thank you' afterwards. Polite, but essentially a complete waste of time and done presumably to prove that he had read the feedback. If the teacher's comments were formative (or, as he would say, negative) he would always write 'I'm sorry. I'll try harder next time.' I did feel quite sad after reading that a number of times. My daughter did no such thing and I put this down to the fact that she has a much more confident sense of herself as a learner than my son does and it showed in his responses. His hold on his confidence as a learner is fragile and it doesn't take too much to convince him that the task at hand is too difficult and well worth quitting. I'll mention a few times in this book that learning needs to be an intrinsically rewarding experience.

Without this sense of satisfaction that comes with the knowledge that you are making progress (and I don't mean in the way we have bastardised the word in teaching these days to mean the next tick on the assessment database that my wife is completing next to me on the sofa as I write this) we can view criticism or feedback as reasons to give up or avoid work altogether.

Your well-intentioned feedback may be taken as scathing criticism

In large part feedback is delivered sensitively by teachers with due regard for the dignity of the child and in the context of a secure, trusting relationship, but there are some avoidable practices that still seem to persist that increase the 'temperature' in relationships and classrooms unnecessarily. Two that trouble me most are:

- Reading out grades and test scores in front of the whole class.
- Public displays ranking students on the basis of attainment.

Nothing good can come from either of these practices. I am ashamed to say that I was guilty of reading out test scores to my Year 10 and Year 11 classes when I first started teaching, largely out of expediency and certainly with no regard to the dignity of the children. Some of the children must have been sitting there dreading the time when their name came up, immediately followed by a number that marked them out as an arbitrary success or failure. Those children just sat there and took it, but some will have hated me for it, others waiting eagerly for public confirmation of their prowess. I see that it is becoming increasingly popular in England for secondary schools to display achievement boards around their site, ranking children on the basis of grades and test scores, with children heading for a hatful of A*s and As at the top and those getting a couple of G or F grades at the bottom. The ham-fisted logic that lauds one child's achievement at the expense of another, and without any regard to their needs or difficulties, is worrying. The child with a learning difficulty who works away at their studies day after day and makes great progress still gets the clear message that they are a failure. The flawed reasoning that we are motivating the children at the bottom of these charts to up their game and get to the top is offensive (see Chapter 5 for more on motivation), as is the assumption behind it which is that their relatively low attainment is simply a result of a lack of effort. I challenge any teachers or leaders employing such tactics to do the same for the staff they manage. Rank them in a big, colourful display based on some arbitrary achievement scale in the staffroom or better, in the reception area, for parents and visitors to see, and set the watch on how long it stays up for. You're on safer ground criticising your partner's driving.

Managing disappointment, getting things wrong and dealing with failure

Have you ever avoided applying for a promotion at school because you convinced yourself that the Headteacher had already made her mind up that Sophie in the Maths Department had the job? Or maybe you know someone else who has done that? This is not behaviour limited to teachers. We protect ourselves with a prophesy that becomes self-fulfilling. We don't put ourselves forward in order to protect ourselves from the painful feelings of rejection. We lie to ourselves by maintaining the certainty that we never stood a chance, so we would be wasting our time even to apply in the first place. If we were honest with ourselves we would admit that it's safer for our ego to avoid the chance of failure altogether than to take the risk that we might actually succeed. I've seen adults, including myself, do this many times and justify to themselves that it is OK, yet it can go unrecognised in schools when children do it or be met with punishment. I will go into more detail on avoidance of failure in Chapter 2 on how psychology can help your understanding, but if we recognised it for what it is and responded accordingly our relationships would be stronger for it.

The late Donald Winnicott, a paediatrician who studied psychoanalysis and did influential work developing the concept of 'holding environments' – that is to say, caring and supporting environments that lead to a firm sense of trust and safety – suggested that it is a duty of parents to slowly but surely disappoint their children; knowing when to say no and being clear with their children that they are not their friend. Substitute 'teacher' for 'parent' above and this still holds true. We are not in this job to indulge children to meet their every whim, but nor are we there to ignore their feelings entirely, in the way I did when I read out test scores to the whole class.

One of the things I loved most when I was a Headteacher was watching my superb colleagues create cultures in their classrooms where mistakes were opportunities to address misconceptions and build on and deepen knowledge. Getting things wrong, struggling and failure were a regular occurrence but the students knew that they would be met with unstinting support and encouragement. We were working with children with learning difficulties – some had been hammering away at their number bonds to 10, 20 or 100, or their initial letter sounds, for a decade, so they were intimately acquainted with feelings of struggle and failure. If mistakes were seen by the children as risks to avoid (and many children came to our school feeling that way) then it is no surprise that work avoidance follows. I summarised to visitors that our students needed to know that *we were there to catch them, not catch them out.*

The best teachers use the errors that children make and the misconceptions they bring to a topic in a positive way, coupled with skilful questioning to deepen the children's knowledge and understanding. You can just ask children if the Earth orbits the Sun or if the Sun orbits the Earth and do a Mrs Rogers on them if they get it wrong (they'll keep guessing until they guess 'correctly'), or you can elicit from them by skilful questioning why they may initially think otherwise and draw them towards what really happens, deepening their understanding of physics in the process. You can achieve some serious depth in a discussion with children when you ask them if a snowman melts quicker or more slowly if you put a coat on him. (Have a think. There is a LOT of physics in this!) Of course, you could just ask them to guess and tell them off if they get it wrong. 'Quicker, er ... I mean slower!' as they look for the subtle cues on your facial expression that indicate if they guessed correctly. In classrooms such as these the children can offer their views, safe in the knowledge that their answer, however wide of the mark, is welcomed and makes a positive contribution to the lesson. They also know, however, that their answer is likely to result in further questioning to elicit the reasoning behind it. Guessing is no good, they need to adopt a position they can defend. A child can maintain that the Earth is flat – a perfectly reasonable conclusion for children given the evidence in front of them – but they can improve their communication skills by defending a position with clarity and precision and improve their reasoning skills if they have to change their mind when the evidence shows that their initial thoughts were, in fact, wrong. Simply telling them otherwise is a missed opportunity. There is an open goal here for children to think hard – and it is a characteristic of classrooms such as these that the children are expected to think hard. (I was introduced to Rosalind Driver et al.'s (1994[9]) excellent book on research into children's ideas about science as a student teacher. I always included a section on lesson plans and schemes of work for common misconceptions about the topics we were covering and this was invaluable. I would deliberately provide opportunities in lessons to cover these, such as the common misconception that there is no gravity on the Moon as it has no atmosphere.) Times such as these improved my communication skills too – try explaining to a child how you can *prove* that the Earth is a sphere or that it orbits the Sun and not the other way round without saying you read it in a book or saw a picture of it!

REFLECTION POINTS

Let's think what might begin to explain work avoidance

Do you work with any children that reject work out of hand before they even begin, or perhaps before they've even seen what it is they'll be doing? Do you work with any children who may even refuse to come into the lesson to begin with? What could be at the heart of that avoidance? Writing? Reading? Speaking? A body image problem (if it's PE)?

Think back to Seanie in the Introduction. Avoiding writing with a paper-thin excuse was preferable to displaying to all who could see that he couldn't write as well as he would like. Any consequence was preferable as it would inevitably involve less or no writing. Mission accomplished.

- How might you approach work avoidance in the future? Are there ways you could pre-empt this happening?

Supporting a successful adult life

I have worked in a broad range of different schools with children with very varying levels of needs, some cognitive, some medical and some behavioural. Some of those children were without a shadow of a doubt going to go on to live and work independently. But some, those with the more significant support needs, had a mountain to climb to achieve full independence in both their personal and working lives and some, sadly, never got there. Part of that independence is the ability to regulate our own emotions and our conduct as soon as we can. Society understands this when we walk past a toddler lying on the floor of the toy shop, crying and screaming that he can't get the toy he wants with the hard-pressed parent doing her or his best to manage the situation, the expectations of the child and resolve the situation without caving in to the child by buying the toy. Society is less forgiving when the person lying on the floor crying and screaming is an adult who is six feet tall and fifteen stone. I often used a memorable but less traumatic example to explain this to visiting parents when they toured my school when I was a Headteacher. For a number of years one of our students, Louise, had a habit of impersonating Alan Sugar.

'You're fired,' she would quip to anyone within sacking distance, delivering the famous *coup de grace* from the reality television show *The Apprentice*.

This was incredibly funny and difficult not to laugh at, yet it became so common that we had to work hard to ensure Louise didn't behave inappropriately and that we didn't encourage her by our responses. We were very successful with this and were feeling very pleased with ourselves. Soon after we were delighted to learn that Louise had been invited to the annual children's Christmas party at 10 Downing Street hosted by the Prime Minister, David Cameron, and his wife, Samantha. Louise was fortunate enough to meet the then Prime Minister and – you can guess what's coming next – the first thing she did was to tell David Cameron that he was fired. On the face of it brilliantly funny, and I'm sure David Cameron was a good sport. However, it feeds the narrative of low expectations from society of some young people, especially those with learning difficulties whom society can infantilise even when they become adults. Louise has Down syndrome and society, in my experience, can infantilise people with this syndrome or with other syndromes or learning difficulties. They expect less from them and allow, either by encouraging or by ignoring, behaviours that they wouldn't accept from people of the same age without special educational needs. In fairness, I'm sure this is, in part, because many people don't actually know the extent of someone's difficulties and, therefore, what it is OK to accept. It's one thing to say that to the Prime Minister on a social occasion, but quite another for it to be your opening remark to anyone and everyone you meet – it becomes a significant barrier to securing employment for starters.

It boils down to this. They've got to be able to manage when they walk out of our schools for the final time and we're not around to support them anymore.

Reducing teacher stress

Last but not least a better understanding of behaviour that leads to improved behaviour will reduce the stress we feel (and, importantly, the stress of the children involved too) as a result. This can only be a good thing.

NASUWT, a large British teaching union, carries out an annual survey called The Big Question. Their 2016 survey,[10] completed by over 12,000 teachers, notes an increase in concerns about behaviour from their 2015 survey. 'Over three quarters (77%) of teachers said that they think there is a widespread behaviour problem in schools today, an increase of 4% from 2015, and over two fifths (44%) said they believe there is a behaviour problem in their schools, an increase of 2% since 2015.'

The survey also notes that 'Over half of teachers (51%) said that they were not given the appropriate training, information and advice to deal with poor pupil behaviour.' Perhaps that's one reason you're reading this book.

Understanding behaviour does matter. It matters for the sake of the child and it matters for the sake of the teacher. Improving our understanding takes an investment in time and energy, but I can assure you that it's worth it. We are the adults in these situations and we need to take responsibility for helping the children understand their own behaviours so that they learn over time to be able to manage without our support, to achieve that independence that they need to be successful adults.

TAKING IT FURTHER – QUESTIONS AND ACTIVITIES FOR YOU AND YOUR COLLEAGUES

- Do we expect our newest children to be school ready, or do we unconditionally welcome them as they are and start from there?
- Do we think about the behavioural development of the children that concern us with the same attention to detail that we give their academic progress?
  - o Consider ways in which you can assess the social and emotional development of these children.
  - o Use this to start using a common language when discussing the development of these children.
- How do we prepare children for planned or short-notice changes to their routines? Do they need more structure, perhaps in the form of visual support, beyond merely telling them?
  - o Consider building in timetable construction to the routine of the start of the day for children for whom changes can be problematic.
- Are we teaching children how to resolve conflicts between themselves? Do we explicitly teach the language and behaviour of conflict resolution? Do we teach the differences between statements, promises and responsibilities?
  - o Consider training up a member of staff to become the resident restorative approaches lead.
- Are some of our feedback policies inadvertently shaming children in public? Can we improve here by considering the dignity of the children and improving our relationships at the same time?
- We all want our classrooms to be, as Winnicott would describe, 'holding environments' – that is to say, caring and supporting environments that lead to a firm sense of trust and safety for everyone in the room. Are there any children who have yet to attain that feeling of security? Can we work out what's missing? What will we need to do to help them feel secure?
- Is failure avoidance behind the behaviour we see for those who seem to avoid certain activities or lessons? If so, how can we reduce the chances of failure?
- Are we over-supporting, leading to a dependence over time from the child towards adults?
- Do we allow some children to display age-inappropriate behaviours, such as hugging, because of their condition or cognitive impairments?

References

1 Biesta, G.J.J. (2015) *Beautiful Rise of Education*. Abingdon: Routledge.
2 https://nurturegroups.org/introducing-nurture/boxall-profile (accessed 11 December 2017).
3 www.fagus.org.uk/ (accessed 11 December 2017).
4 Blair, C. and Raver, C.C. (2015) 'School readiness and self-regulation: a developmental psychobiological approach', *Annual Review of Psychology*, 66: 711–31. doi:10.1146/annurev-psych-010814-015221.
5 Blair, C. and Razza, R.P. (2007) 'Relating effortful control, executive function, and false belief understanding to emerging math and literacy ability in kindergarten', *Child Development*, 78(2): 647–63.
6 Burchinal, M.R., Peisner-Feinberg, E.S., Bryant, D.M. and Clifford, R.M. (2000) 'Children's social and cognitive development and child care quality: testing for differential associations related to poverty, gender, or ethnicity', *Applied Developmental Science*, 4 (3): 149–65.
7 https://drlindagraham.wordpress.com/2016/03/30/acknowledging-the-little-things/ (accessed 14 December 2017).
8 Rogers, B. (2002) *Classroom Behaviour: A Practical Guide to Effective Teaching, Behaviour Management and Colleague Support*. London: Paul Chapman Publishing.
9 Driver, R., Squires, A., Rushworth, P. and Wood-Robinson, V. (1994) *Making Sense of Secondary Science: Research into Children's Ideas*. Abingdon: Routledge.
10 NASUWT. *The Big Question 2016*. www.nasuwt.org.uk/uploads/assets/uploaded/c316d25b-d8d7-4595-bbb0f9181d0427d1.pdf (accessed 11 December 2017).

2

HOW PSYCHOLOGY CAN HELP YOUR UNDERSTANDING

Schools work best when adults believe in children and children believe
they believe in them.

Dave Whitaker, Executive Principal,
Springwell Learning Community

THE HEADLINES

- Children need to be accepted into your classroom and your care
  unconditionally.

- Understand that the children are attempting to deal with situations in
  their lives as best they can.

- If, despite doing their *best*, they are not doing *well*, look at what skills
  they need in order for them to do well.

- Know that in any behaviour situation there are two problems to be
  solved – your problem and the child's problem. Yours will be easier to
  identify and to find solutions for.

- The solution(s) to these problems needs to be mutually beneficial.

- Negative behaviour communicates an unmet need and is an attempt to
  have those needs met.

- Emotional investment is characterised by children feeling valued by
  adults, of being regarded as significant and of having a stake or a
  sense of belonging in their school/class/year group/house.

- For those who feel rejected, isolated or invisible it is easy to feel that
  they don't matter.

- Avoid negative thoughts that lead to emotional responses that influence
  your behaviour (faulty thinking) such as:
  - predicting failure;
  - ignoring positives and focusing on negatives;
  - putting children in unwinnable positions;

- o   labelling children (i.e. unteachable);
    - o   defining yourself as powerless.
- Recognise that we over-emphasise personal characteristics as the reasons for someone's behaviour and under-emphasise or ignore the context in which the behaviour occurs.
- Positive expectations have a positive influence on performance.
- Negative expectations have a negative influence on performance.

The psychology of human behaviour deserves a library all of its own and as such one chapter in one book cannot hope to cover the entire field. However, an understanding of a few key concepts can make a big difference to how you think about the behaviour of children in your classes and, crucially, about your own behaviour. Some of these concepts I learned about after I had developed a certain way of thinking and others commented that it reminded them of someone or other: 'Do you know the work of Carl Rogers? You should read some of his work as your approach chimes with much of what he thought.'

They gave me the confidence that I wasn't the only one thinking that way and helped me to firstly set my thoughts within some psychological frame-work and then to extend them further and make me think more deeply. Others I found, sometimes out of desperation, when I was faced with a big problem and didn't know which way to turn, such as Aaron Beck's work on faulty thinking. I also learned a lot about behaviour from my time as a Special Constable with Thames Valley Police. We had far more training on behaviour and psychology when I was a recruit and it brought into sharp relief the paucity of behaviour training I received both as a trainee teacher and when I became qualified. Obvious in many ways I suppose, given that police officers deal with more extreme behaviours more often and with adults as well as children, some under the influence of one or more sub-stances. However, the skills I learned as a police officer made me a far better teacher in terms of managing the behaviour of a class of children. My aim with this chapter is to provide you with some psychological principles and theories that will help you to understand the behaviour of children in your classes, how you can support them and also get you thinking about your own behaviour in readiness for Chapter 3 on precisely that topic.

Unconditional positive regard

Unconditional positive regard is a concept developed by Carl Rogers (1902–87), a humanistic psychologist. His concept led me to realise that I had significantly underestimated that the attitude I adopted to the children who walked in to my classroom was a principal determinant in how well they behaved.

A complete and unconditional acceptance of each child in your class for who they are and what they do is the bedrock of any work to improve behaviour. Without this, children are only accepted under certain conditions that you or the school get to decide (conditions that may well be unknown to the child) and this positive regard is withdrawn when the child behaves in ways that breach those conditions.

Unconditional positive regard means accepting that the child is attempting to deal with situations in their lives as best they can. Is their behaviour inappropriate? Maybe. Is it destructive? Possibly. But at least you start from where the child is at and seek to improve from that position rather than resorting to the tired and ineffective punishment escalator, bemoaning that children don't respect adults any more and that they didn't behave this way when you were a kid.

I place this concept first in this chapter because it is the foundation of everything that is to follow. Without an unconditional acceptance of each and every child you cannot hope to understand what is going on in front of you.

REFLECTION POINTS

- Do you begin lessons with comments such as 'If I see the behaviour I had from you yesterday then there'll be trouble'?

- Are there conditions for the acceptance of children in your class or school?

- If so, are those conditions different for different children?

Lagging skills and unmet needs

Dr Ross Greene is an American clinical psychologist who contends that children will do well if they can. Central to Greene's contention is that if someone is not doing well it is because they lack the necessary skills to be successful at that point ('lagging skills' as Greene calls them). I like this way of thinking a lot. It makes sense to me that no one sets out to be unsuccessful, to fail, to potentially embarrass themselves in front of their peers and their teachers. (I will mention below in a bit more detail the potential difference between what you define as doing well in any particular situation and what the child defines as doing well.)

If you disagree with the proposition that children will do well if they can, you are likely to be working on the assumption that children will do well if they choose (that word again). This is endemic in teaching and that is why teachers reach time and again for punishments and rewards because behaving well becomes for them a simple matter of choice and changing that behaviour is an equally simple matter of incentivising and motivating the child (see Chapter 5 for more on this). Unfortunately teachers have to reach for it time and again because it is ineffective.

Greene sees skills gaps as problems to be solved collaboratively as opposed to traditional behavioural interventions which are done to children, not with them. You must be alert, though, to the fact that there are probably two problems in the mix that need to be identified and solved – the child's and your own. Your problem – the child refusing to enter your classroom, say – has an obvious solution which rests entirely with the child. 'Just do as I ask and the problem goes away.' Identifying the child's problem will take more work and is probably only going to be achieved by talking to them. With younger children and/or those with communication difficulties this may prove more challenging but is, I would argue, even more important. As Joe Bower (2012) says, 'The child must feel like you care about solving their problem as much as you care about solving your own.'[1]

It follows that once we identify problems we aim for solutions. Greene's method calls for collaborative solutions that solve both the child's problem and yours. You can see that this is not straightforward because adults or children can suggest solutions that are unworkable. The child may want a different teacher or you may want the child to simply comply despite the fact they cannot read the textbook they're working from. Ross Greene writes that this 'model is non-punitive and non-adversarial, decreases the likelihood of conflict, enhances relationships, improves communication, and helps kids and adults learn and display the skills on the more positive side of human nature: empathy, appreciating how one's behavior is affecting others, resolving disagreements in ways that do not involve conflict, taking another's perspective, and honesty'.[2] I am sure that old school traditionalists would rather lose a limb than work in such a way and be seen to give ground to children, but I am afraid that they will be stuck in the cycle of doling out punishments until the naughty children see the error of their ways. To learn more about this approach look up Greene's Assessment of Lagging Skills and Unsolved Problems (ALSUP).[3]

With Greene's thinking in mind, I have settled on a way of looking at problems myself. I view negative behaviour as the communication of an unmet need. Negative as perceived by the adult, of course. The child may say it was necessary, desirable even, but if it is disruptive to learning then of course it is problematic. No matter what the child's behaviour, and no matter how dangerous it is, we should understand it for what it is – an attempt to have their needs met. This does not mean that we condone it or that the behaviour is appropriate or even effective. For example, if my children are in danger then I will do whatever it takes to keep them safe. The law and whatever is deemed socially appropriate cease to be important to me at this time. I will simply do whatever it takes to have my needs met which, in this case, is to ensure the safety of my children. These needs override any consideration of potential consequences.

As a result I understand that all behaviour is the right behaviour. Right in the sense that the child has chosen, consciously or subconsciously, to behave in a certain way in response to the situation they find themselves in. Telling a teacher to fuck off is not appropriate and is unlikely to be effective (unless 'effective' is defined as getting out of your class in which case it may be highly effective, but still inappropriate), but the child has selected that course of action for a reason. This is where Ross Greene's concept of lagging skills comes in. There are likely to be a number of courses of action open to a child that would have been more effective, so consider why that course of action was chosen and if it resulted from a skills gap as Greene would say.

To round up, I will use an example from my own life. I have a visceral hatred of singing and dancing in public. I am not good at either of them; they make me feel very self-conscious and I get this overwhelming feeling that everyone is looking at me and laughing at my ineptitude. These are some of my lagging skills and I am perfectly fine with the fact that I am a poor singer and dancer. I see no value in either skill for me so I have no motivation to want to improve. I am in the fortunate position to be able to avoid doing either of them and people generally don't try to make me do them either, especially people who know me well. However, if I am cornered and forced into a position then things are definitely going to take a turn for the worse. You may plan a training session in which you're planning for the delegates to sing or dance (I have been in one INSET where it became sickeningly apparent to me as time passed that this was going to happen). Remember, children ⌜Jarlath⌝ will do well if they can, but in my case doing well will be defined as doing everything in my power to avoid doing what you want me to do. My clear need here is to avoid embarrassing myself and if that need is unmet then my behaviour will communicate this to you. I will try desperately to avoid being rude, but if you force the issue I will invent a reason, such as a phone call, to escape. I may resort to being rude by simply refusing to take part. You can threaten me as much as you like, but sanctions or consequences are likely to be preferable for me because they won't involve singing or dancing. Mission accomplished. You can offer to reward me as much as you like, but no inducement will alleviate my embarrassment. I may, if the inducement is big enough, do the absolute bare minimum, but I certainly won't put my heart and soul into it and my initial problem remains unsolved afterwards and will rear its head again next time.

Problem solve with me. Your problem is that I won't sing or dance. My problem is not that I hate singing or dancing. My problem is that I hate the public embarrassment and the feelings of self-consciousness that flow from singing and dancing in public (don't be seduced into thinking that the superficial issue is the problem, it probably isn't). Work with me to alleviate that. Allow me to do it in private. Give me a route out that preserves my dignity yet allows me to be successful, to feel like I am making progress and I am all yours. Our next session will go better too.

For me it is singing and dancing in public. For some of the children we work with it may be reading, handwriting, answering questions in front of the class, sensory problems, friendship and social issues, or a range of other anxieties. Identifying the underlying lagging skills will set you on the road to solving both their problem and yours together.

REFLECTION POINTS

Next time you work through a behaviour issue:

- Ask yourself why this child can't currently do well in this situation.
- Ask what needs are going unmet in this situation.
- Use Greene's ALSUP to identify lagging skills.
- Identify *your* problem to be solved.
- Identify *their* problem to be solved.
- Ensure the solution works for both of you.

Emotional investment

I was first introduced to the concept of emotional investment after a particularly unsavoury incident one lunchtime in the school I worked at for children with emotional and behavioural difficulties (EBD). Lunch was a communal affair with all staff and students eating together every day and this was a great way to deepen relationships and teach social skills. We had breakfast together too before school for the same reasons. One student, Drew, had recently returned to the school after a few years away and was refusing to follow an instruction from the Headteacher. He was very quietly but firmly asked to leave the dining room for a period of time but was resolute in his determination to stay (in order to save face presumably). It became a very uncomfortable public stand-off. After a few seconds that felt like hours Drew got up, turned over a table and shouted 'Fuck you, you fucking blonde bimbo!' and walked out. Admirably, the Headteacher carried on lunchtime as normal for everyone else. Once they were all settled she went to see him, he came back in and had his lunch. Each day after school we had a staff debrief and this incident was top of the agenda for that day. Some staff were unhappy. 'You allowed Drew talk to you like that in front of everyone else!' 'You let him get away with it!' The Headteacher politely listened then said, 'I asked Drew to leave the room. He left the room. He did what I asked him to do. Am I happy with *how* he left the room? No. I ignored his secondary behaviour [the swearing] and I dealt with it afterwards away from an audience. Drew knows he has to repair the situation with me and with the rest of the school which he will do tomorrow. Remember, he has no emotional investment in this school. He has just arrived. Relationships here have no value to him. *Yet*. He has no respect for the school. *Yet*.' The penny dropped for me at that moment. The Headteacher was talking about something we sometimes call 'buy-in'. Drew hadn't bought in to our way of working or our ethos yet and it showed.

To me emotional investment is characterised by you giving a part of yourself to someone, something or somewhere and receiving some form of sustenance in return (I like to think of this as the dividend). It is positively reinforcing in that the greater the investment generally the greater the dividend and people are more likely to act in ways to protect or grow that investment over time. But, of course, investment is risky ('stocks may go up or may go down' as the smallprint on the adverts say) and not everyone starts with a nil balance. Some children arrive at your school having left another school in difficult circumstances. They will be wary of investing anything in you as they are anticipating rejection – the response they have become used to. That's why we have to make the initial outlay – we need to be the ones who invest in the child first. We have to help them resist the urge to quit on their own terms. This is mutually beneficial as your demonstrable commitment to understanding and helping that child starts to build the feelings of belonging, security and confidence. They can start to trust you and invest in you. The balance starts to build; then, and only then, if they do go through a rocky period – everyone does – they will be better placed to manage. Strong relationships withstand tough times and repairing them when they are damaged becomes a priority for the child.

There are an infinite number of ways to build emotional investment. Every time you run an extra revision session, every time you call home with good news, every time you volunteer to have your legs waxed on stage for Sixth Form fund-raising week (twice, for the record, without an epidural), every time you take the trouble to ask how their dog is because it was at the vets last week, you're building. You're building up your own emotional investment in the place and the people in it, and the bond with the people you work with too grows stronger. But be warned, I am not asking you to martyr yourself here. Goodness knows us teachers are all give, give, give, so pay close attention to ensure you've got enough left at the end of the week for you and your own family.

REFLECTION POINTS

- Do the children feel valued in your class? A feeling of significance or of having a stake is an important part of being invested in a place.

- Perhaps they feel rejected, isolated or invisible? It is much harder to feel that you matter if you feel you aren't valued.

- Do the children in your class have a sense of belonging? This could be to their tutor group (the most important job in a secondary school in my view, and the one I loved the most), the school cricket team or their house, for example. A feeling of identity is an important part of being invested in a place.

Faulty thinking (aka cognitive distortion)

I first became interested in the work of Dr Aaron Beck, an American psychoanalytic therapist, when I became a Headteacher in 2011. Beck did some very influential work in the 1960s on depression and was seeking to recognise negative thoughts that led to emotional responses. Beck applied these concepts to the ways that people thought about themselves and their own situations, yet the ways of thinking strike me as very powerful when we apply them to how we as teachers think about the children we teach and their behaviour. Before I became a Headteacher I viewed the attitude of teachers towards individual children as simply either positive or negative. It was only when I had the privilege of leading a school and trying to improve the behaviour of the children that I thought about it in any more depth. I had to, as I had to have uncomfortable conversations with colleagues to challenge them when I observed negativity creeping in. Uncomfortable as it will undoubtedly be, challenge them you must. If we are to improve the behaviour of the children we work with then we must firstly eradicate this way of thinking and then have the courage to challenge colleagues if they do the same. Then and only then can we claim to have the right culture in our schools. Read Dave Whitaker's quote at the beginning of this chapter again and you will see that negativity in all its forms is incompatible with building schools that feel right. Challenging each other is not something that we as a profession like to do, but it happened all the time when I was a police officer. 'I challenge that' was a phrase I heard often in the station and it was common for officers to debrief situations with each other robustly. This makes sense as the consequences of poor practice in the police could be catastrophic, such as the escape of an offender, the destruction of some evidence, the injury of a fellow officer or victim or far, far worse. This gave a strong motivation to colleagues to address issues there and then. The consequences in teaching for calling a child 'a nightmare' aren't so immediately serious, but they are damaging and a failure to challenge allows a culture to creep in that can be extremely difficult to undo. Believe me, I've been there.

I will explore below the main elements of faulty thinking, how they might manifest themselves in your classroom (and in your head) and what you can do to stop them. I confess to having committed each and every one of the following at some stage in my teaching life. How about you?

1. Predicting failure – aka The Fortune Teller Error

'Great. He's going to destroy my lesson today.'

This comment, dripping with passive aggression, was aimed at me in a daily staff briefing by a colleague after I had informed our team that Joe was returning to school on that day. Joe was a serial absentee and, when he was in school, all of us found it difficult at times to help him behave well. The comment immediately raised my hackles and I responded in a slightly more pointed manner than I should have done. 'Well, if that's your attitude then he probably will,' spilled out of my mouth immediately. The comment irritated me because my colleague had already decided how her lesson would pan out. She had predicted failure – something that teachers must be immune from. It is one thing to know that a child is currently experiencing difficulties in managing to behave well; it is another thing altogether to decide that they won't. Not 'can't', 'won't' – there's a world of difference. One brings with it the responsibility and commitment to plan to support the child – 'We always plan for success' as a colleague of mine for many years would often say – the other decides that there is nothing you as the teacher can do. This is such a disempowering attitude to adopt as you deem yourself powerless.

Prediction of failure can manifest itself in more ways than the blatant example above. Look out for examples such as:

> Excluding a child from an activity such as a trip, a residential or a school play because someone believes the child won't manage. Ask what support will need to be put in place to make it successful.

Restricting curriculum access to certain children. I know of a number of secondary schools that have a number of different option booklets that they hand out to students when choosing their Key Stage 4 subjects. This means that some students are restricted in their choice of subjects – a policy that I think is indefensible. Presumably this is done in an attempt to improve the school's chances of doing well in overall performance measures, but it places children as unwitting pawns in a game of school standards chess.

2. Ignoring positives and focusing on negatives

'Olivia just can't do anything right this week.'

Focusing on things that haven't gone well and ignoring or failing to notice things that have is a common enough trait in teachers as we apply it to ourselves frequently. Think of all the times you have received feedback on a lesson observation from a colleague – if you are like me you will have honed in on the criticisms and forgotten the things that they said went well.

But it can unfortunately be applied to the children we teach too. This kind of thinking maintains negative beliefs despite the fact that they may be contradicted by the actual evidence of how a child's conduct has been when viewed across the whole school. This can be reinforced in a secondary school environment where we are almost certain to see only a partial picture of a child's time in school which we then extend to be true for all other teachers and times of the day.

Bill Rogers uses the image of the black dot in the white square to represent this. The black dot represents something negative that has caught your focus and the white square surrounding it is all the good stuff that is happening. What do you focus on? The black dot obviously, but you have to fight against that urge.

This is also a surefire way for children to develop a reputation in the staffroom. If you only ever hear about the problems a child has caused to certain teachers – and some of us are louder and more dominant in staffrooms than others – a narrative builds up about that child that can be hard to break down. It's in our nature to let off steam in the staffroom but if we continually talk down certain children the Pygmalion effect kicks in (see below).

3. All-or-nothing

'Dina, you have to be perfect for the rest of the term or else you can't go on the class trip.'

All-or-nothing thinking places children (especially if they have had behavioural difficulties) in an almost unwinnable position by demanding perfection from them or else they fail. The faulty thinking comes about because we think that we can extrinsically motivate a child to hold it together for the trip, or other activity considered desirable for the child, and, therefore, assume that prior negative behaviour was just a simple pre-meditated choice to be naughty. All we need to do is to offer the child something tantalising (like a trip), but give them no margin of error in order to be successful. The logic is that the stakes are so high that the child sorts themselves out to avoid failure – that'll make them focus! Simple, but fatally flawed. To make matters worse, we don't impose these unattainable expectations on the rest of the class. This child has to work harder than the rest of the class, despite their difficulties. We resort to this kind of despera-tion for the children who have found it hardest to be successful under our normal conditions, so raising the height of the hurdle to jump over is doomed to failure.

Helping colleagues understand the impossible position the child has been placed in can allow them to readjust. Also, remember that if the trip or other activity the child looks forward to, like swimming for example, is part of the curriculum it should never be offered conditionally. We don't do this with tests or maths – 'Dina, you have to be perfect for the rest of the term or else you can't do the end-of-unit test,' said no teacher ever.

4. Labelling

'Leo is a total nightmare.'

Labelling, also more accurately known as mislabelling in my view, uses very strong and emotionally loaded language to generalise about a child. When we refer to a child as a nightmare or as one of the naughty ones we're doing this. You might think that referring to a child as naughty is pretty harmless, but the child then becomes the behaviour – they become 'unmanageable' as opposed to the behaviour being unmanageable (no behaviour is unmanage-able, by the way, but I hear the word used often enough). 'We don't label children or families in this school. Separate the behaviour from the child,' you might say to challenge.

5. Fallacy of control

'Nothing works with this class.'

This is a form of self-emasculation whereby we define ourselves as helpless and at the mercy of fate or of others, including the children or the senior leadership team. It weakens our position as we feel little or no ability to influence, change and, therefore, improve behaviour. The worst of this is that we can simply stop trying. We come to dread the lessons with this class or child approaching and, like with the prediction of failure above, expect the worst. In these cases it is support that is needed, not challenge, and lots of it. If a colleague feels this helpless then this is where we pile in with as much support as we can muster to turn that situation around. I think I was in this situation when I described in the Introduction the time I sought support from a senior leader and was thrown one of Rob Long's pamphlets. It is not a nice place to be, but it is hard to recognise in yourself that you're there.

REFLECTION POINTS

- What kind of comments do you hear in the staffroom that suggest ways of faulty thinking described above?
- What could you say to colleagues when you hear this negativity?
- How could you support them to think differently?

---

6. The fundamental attribution error

'Well, my son never behaves like that at home!'

Ever heard that one? Of course you have and you've probably said it too if you're a parent. Are we *really* that surprised that children (this applies to everyone, including teachers, actually) behave differently at home to the way they do at school? We shouldn't be; they behave differently within school with different teachers so of course they behave differently outside of school. I think, deep down, all of us get this, but there's a deeper problem at the root of this. It is that we tend to over-emphasise the reasons for another person's behaviour as being down to their attitudes or their personal characteristics and under-emphasise or ignore the situation, the context or the environment in which the person is behaving and which is placing demands on them. Social psychologist Lee Ross (1977) calls this the fundamental attribution error[4] and psychologist Dr Richard Nisbett (2015) contends that this is the 'most pervasive and consequential inferential mistake we make'.[5] He says that '[T]here is vastly more going on in our heads than we realise … Pay more attention to context. This will improve the odds that you'll correctly identify situational factors that are influencing your behavior and that of others … Realize that situational factors usually influence your behavior and that of others more than they seem to, whereas dispositional factors are usually less influential than they seem.' As Dr Tim O'Brien (2015) (no relation) says in his excellent *Inner Story* 'Your behaviour is a result of what you bring to an environment and what an environment brings to you.'[6]

Perhaps you've heard colleagues tell you that children with ADHD just can't sit still. Of course they can, but there will be situations in your classroom where a child with ADHD might find it more difficult to sit still. There is a big difference between the two. Knowing how best to support that child and how best to set up your classroom, present your resources and conduct yourself (the situational factors) will give that child the best possible chance of succeeding.

It is a form of labelling, to use Beck's term discussed above, and is a very limiting way of thinking. We give children innate, unchangeable one-word descriptors such as 'naughty', 'unteachable' or 'rude' and this becomes their defining characteristic. No child is rude all of the time or to everyone that they meet and a failure to take account of context risks missing why they have been rude in a particular instance. At the risk of sounding like a broken record, this does not mean that their rudeness in that instance was acceptable or that we should do nothing about it. Quite the opposite in fact, but to go down this road means an inevitable moment when we decide that there is nothing we can do (the fallacy of control, remember) – this child is quite simply naughty and that's that. Always has been. Always will be.

I said earlier in the chapter that we should understand behaviour as a child's attempts to have their needs met. When thought of that way, all behaviour is the right behaviour. It follows, therefore, that the need is not innate to the child (the dispositional factors), it is in response to the child's interaction with other people and with their environment (the situational factors). It could be fear, boredom, noise or love, for example, and these emotions are created by the interaction between the child and his or her environment and the other people around the child. The child must be scared of something or someone; they must be bored of something or someone. They cannot simply be scared or bored. With this in mind it becomes more natural to think of negative behaviour as the communication of an unmet need and to then think about how you can best support that child with those needs. To reinforce the point made earlier, this does not mean that the behaviour is acceptable or even effective. The unmet need may involve them wanting to put as much distance between themselves and you as possible, for example. This doesn't make it OK, but it allows you to understand why they are doing what they are doing and you can work on changing the situation to make things better.

The Pygmalion effect

Just as we have a tendency to think that the reasons for behavioural problems are more about the person than about the context, there is a danger that we lower or raise our expectations of the individual children in our class depending on the judgements we make about them. You may think that you wouldn't do such a thing, but research suggests that we can make this error. Research by psychologists Robert Rosenthal and Lenore Jacobsen (1968) showed that the expectations of teachers influence the performance of their students.[7] As you would hope, positive expectations have a positive influence on the performance of your students, but the flip side quite clearly is that negative expectations influence performance negatively. Rosenthal and Jacobsen described this phenomenon as the Pygmalion effect, saying 'when we expect certain behaviors of others, we are likely to act in ways that make the expected behavior more likely to occur'. We all like to believe that we have nothing but the highest expectations for all of our students, so let's look at what this might actually mean in a classroom.

The most common form I see of the Pygmalion effect in terms of behaviour is when adults escalate certain situations with some children that they wouldn't with others. 'Why on Earth would an adult do that?' you may ask. It's a good question but I've seen it many times. One of the things that I try to impress upon people when I provide training on behaviour is that we should never escalate a situation – a teachers' version of the medical profession's 'First, do no harm'. We can escalate by infringement chasing or by reacting more vigorously to secondary behaviours. There are some children that some teachers are itching to catch out. One thing, the shirt untucked let's say, then leads on to the forgotten pen, the missed homework, the odd expletive uttered in the playground, behaviour dragged up from last week. I've seen these same infringements dealt with very differently depending on which child is committing them. For some who very rarely step over the behaviour line the untucked shirt is dealt with quietly, or ignored altogether interestingly, whereas for others it is the beginning of a stream of errors the teacher points out to the whole class and yet further proof that the child just isn't up to it and is pounced upon with punishment. Again.

The Pygmalion effect research is backed up by the work of John Darley and Paget Gross (1983), psychologists at Princeton University, who carried out an experiment in which students made stereotypical judgements about a child based on their judgement of her social class.[8] The experiment contended that '[p]eople will expect and demand less of [working-class Hannah], and they will perceive her performance as being worse than if she were upper middle class'. This chimes with the kind of comment I've heard quite a few times in my nearly two decades as a teacher – *'Well, what do you expect from kids from that family?'*

You will have noticed that there is much common ground here with Aaron Beck's work on faulty thinking. It essentially amounts to us, the well-trained professional, unwittingly or otherwise, creating a playing field with a gradient that is favourable for some children and leg-sappingly steep for others. We must be alert to our tendency to think this way and to work against it to ensure we don't disadvantage those children for whom school can already be a difficult place to feel successful.

Defeating destiny

I was fortunate to listen to Graham Donaldson, former Her Majesty's Chief Inspector of Education in Scotland, speak in 2016 in Swansea on his work on Welsh curriculum reform. He explained that, given the poor life outcomes for some children, he felt that a major aim of the work was 'defeating destiny'. I was lucky to be speaking after him and let him know that from that moment on I would be using that phrase as it encapsulated perfectly what I felt those of us working with children with special educational needs were trying to do. I strongly feel that the phrase applies equally well to our work with children who sometimes struggle to behave well in schools. Some have been on the punishment escalator for years and there is no sign that they will step off any time soon. The go-to punishments of detentions and exclusions do not work for them and, indeed, many simply factor them into their school lives. Their futures have been mapped out for them, sometimes because we have written them off and publicly declared them to be beyond help, either in the staff-room or to their face. This is why lessons from psychology can help us to change our own attitude, to look deeper to the communication of unmet needs and to seek to address the skills gaps that will help these children behave better. To reiterate Ross Greene's mantra, 'children do well if they can'. It is our duty to help them to learn to do well. Only then can we defeat destiny.

TAKING IT FURTHER – QUESTIONS AND ACTIVITIES FOR YOU AND YOUR COLLEAGUES

- Have a discussion with colleagues about what unconditional positive regard looks and sounds like in your school or classroom.

- When discussing behavioural issues ask yourselves the following questions:
  o What needs is the child trying to meet by behaving in this way?
  o Does the child know what it means to do well in this situation?
  o What skills does the child need to do well in this situation?

(Continued)

- o Can we identify what we need to do to support the child to improve those skills?
- o Does the solution we propose meet both our needs and that of the child?
- o Are we resisting working in this way as we feel we are giving ground to the child? (Think unconditional positive regard here.)
- o Are we trying to win? If so, do we recognise that the child won't like losing?

- In what ways does our school promote emotional investment?
  - o Do we have an active and vibrant house system?
  - o Do we celebrate progress, not just high attainment?
  - o Do we have any invisible children?
  - o Do we inadvertently make some children feel that they matter less than others?
  - o Do our children feel that they are significant, that they are important?
  - o How do we demonstrate this?
  - o What do the children say when we ask them?

- Do we have the courage to challenge negativity in each other when we hear it or see it?
  - o Do we predict failure?
  - o Do we ignore positives?
  - o Do we focus on negatives?

- Make an agreement between colleagues that you will politely, but firmly, remind each other if you come across negativity. Use an agreed script to make this less difficult – 'We don't predict failure in this school, Mr Hill. Tell me about something that went well today.'

- Eliminate the prediction of failure by focusing on what support will be required for that child to be successful.

- When discussing behavioural issues focus heavily on the context around which the behaviour occurred. Fight the urge to simply put it down to the presence of that particular child. It is the interaction between the child, other people and their environment that is important, not simply the child themselves.

References

1   http://joe-bower.blogspot.co.uk/2012/04/collaborative-problem-solving.html (accessed 11 December 2017).
2   http://drrossgreene.com/about-cps.htm (accessed 11 December 2017).
3   www.livesinthebalance.org/paperwork (accessed 11 December 2017).

4   Ross, L. (1977) 'The intuitive psychologist and his shortcomings: distortions in the attribution process', in L. Berkowitz (ed.), *Advances in Experimental Social Psychology*. New York: Academic Press. pp. 173–220.

5   Nisbett, R. (2015) *Mindware: Tools for Smart Thinking*. London: Penguin. pp. 48–9.

6   O'Brien, T. (2015) *Inner Story: Understand Your Mind: Change Your World*. CreateSpace.

7   Rosenthal, R. and Jacobsen, L. (1968) *Pygmalion in the Classroom: Teacher Expectation and Pupils' Intellectual Development*. New York: Holt, Rinehart and Winston. And see also Rosenthal, R. and Babad, E.Y. (1985) 'Pygmalion in the gymnasium', *Educational Leadership*, 43 (1): 36–9.

8   Darley, J.M. and Gross, P.H. (1983) 'A hypothesis-confirming bias in labelling effects', *Journal of Personality and Social Psychology*, 44 (1): 20–33.

3

YOUR BEHAVIOUR

I've come to a frightening conclusion that I am the decisive element in the classroom. It's my personal approach that creates the climate. It's my daily mood that makes the weather. As a teacher, I possess a tremendous power to make a child's life miserable or joyous. I can be a tool of torture or an instrument of inspiration. I can humiliate or heal. In all situations, it is my response that decides whether a crisis will be escalated or de-escalated and a child humanized or dehumanized.

Haim Ginott

THE HEADLINES

- Your first task in any situation is to ensure that your behaviour does not escalate the situation.

- Treating every day as a fresh start is not simply a cliché. It is vital as our relationships must withstand the bad times.

- Some children experience, and indeed expect, failure and rejection on a regular basis. Our behaviour can show them that we are safe people to be around and that we want them to be successful.

- When children sabotage situations to avoid failure or challenge, our behaviour can show them that they are welcomed back unconditionally.

- It is important to recognise in yourself the times when your capacity to cope with poor behaviour is compromised.

- Courtesy is contagious – modelling the behaviour we want from our children is vital.

- Your voice is immensely powerful. Talk to the children as if their parents were sat next to them.

- Sometimes our behaviours as adults indicate a desire to win, and that means that a child has to lose.

Say the word 'behaviour' in the context of schools and every single one of us will automatically think of the behaviour of children. We have a justified obsession as a profession with the behaviour of the children we work with and you can be sure as a topic of staffroom conversation it is in a constant tussle for the top spot with criticism of our bosses, sometimes joining together like a pair of mutually orbiting supermassive black holes when talking about how terrible our bosses are at sorting out behaviour. How often do we talk about our own behaviour and examine the effect it has on the children we work with? Have you ever escalated a situation because of your behaviour that, with hindsight, you could have handled much better? I'll be amazed if you haven't. I certainly have, I'm sorry to say. We need to critically examine our own conduct in our classrooms and devote more dis-cussion to it both in the staffroom and in training sessions as it is a vital ingredient in improving behaviour and this is why a chapter on this topic appears here.

I don't recall my own behaviour ever being explicitly mentioned in my teacher training, but it formed a major element to my regular training as a Special Constable. I worked with lots of different officers in my time with Thames Valley Police, but one particular officer, Brendan, was one of the finest for one major reason. The first thing he said to me when we were crewed together to search for a missing person has stayed with me ever since. 'I aim to get to retirement without ever having to use this [points to his baton] or this [points to his pepper spray] by using this [points to his mouth] and these [points to his ears].' I immediately warmed to him. It reminded me of Professor Paul Black (best known for his work on formative assessment with Dylan Wiliam) who said at a conference I was fortunate enough to be at that 'Teachers should have bigger ears and smaller mouths.' How, and how much, we use the natural tools at our disposal can drastically affect both how the people we're working with respond and react to us and how those situations and our relationships improve or deteriorate.

I had worked with my brother, Pete, himself a full-time police officer, plenty of times and seen him expertly use his communication skills to de-escalate situations that could easily have got out of hand and knew for sure, just like Haim Ginott above, that we were the decisive element in any situation. I had also seen officers escalate situations when flexing their power unnecessarily. Once, a crewmate and I had stopped and searched a man in the street and my colleague checked over the radio to see if he was currently wanted by us or any another constabulary. This man had been through the drill many times before and knew what was happening, but the tension was still there all the same. The control room would let my crewmate know through the earpiece connected to his radio (which I could also hear, but the man could not) if there was a warrant out for his arrest. 'He is known to us, but not currently wanted,' came through, meaning we could let him go. My crewmate, instead of letting this man go on his way, grabbed him by the upper arm, put his face in the man's, who was waiting anxiously, remember, to find out if he was to be imminently arrested, and said 'I'm sorry to tell you that … you can go,' then gently pushed him away, laughing smugly. For a second I was sure he was going to punch my crewmate. Instead, the man thought better of it, let out a big sigh and then walked off, muttering something inaudible under his breath that was probably remarkably similar to the words running through my head at the same time. I was inexperienced and lacked the courage to talk this situation through with my crewmate, which is something that I still regret. I know that it made my fellow officer feel big and powerful, but it worried me. Police officers met this man regularly because he was a prolific car thief, so next time he could be more defensive and edgy, making his responses unpredictable and increasing the chances of someone getting hurt and him getting arrested again for something completely avoidable. Yes, that was one officer, but a negative interaction with one officer can easily extend to tarring all police officers with the same brush.

Police officers and teachers do radically different jobs yet there are clear similarities in how we set the tone in our interactions with the people with whom we work. There are key differences – teachers work with the same people every day (few relationships between a police officer and a member of the general public extend to more than one interaction). Our relationships with the children we work with must withstand the bad times. We've all got to get on with the next lesson and the next day irrespective of how the previous lesson or day has gone. Crucially, do not lose sight of the fact that this is also true for the child, perhaps even more so, for they have to re-enter what they will consider to be your domain. Even if they have been in your class in primary school, say, for more than one year, it is still regarded by them as *your* classroom. This is why it is important for us to regard every day as a fresh start, and to really mean it. For sure, an incident that happens on one day may well end up being dealt with the next day for various reasons, but we should not bring up past misdemeanours as a way of rubbing a child's face in it. Beginning a new day with 'Today had better be an improvement on yesterday's disaster or else,' is unnecessary and likely to be counter-productive. That fraction of a second when your gaze first meets theirs as they walk through your door the next time after an incident will set the tone for that lesson because they will be alert to all the subtle clues you will be giving off, just as you will be alert to theirs. In that instant without saying a word or uttering a noise you can communicate to a child if they are welcomed back or not. Such is the power of your body language.

We share the ability with police officers to colour the views of one person about all members of our school or our profession by our personal behaviour. All schools can come to be regarded as unsafe places to be, a particular subject can be considered to be impossible or all teachers regarded as unsafe people to be around on the basis of one bad experience. Just listen to the number of parents, perhaps the mistakenly called 'hard-to-reach', who return to their own decades-old negative experience of schooling. A rawness can remain like a scar that reminds us of a nasty childhood accident. The beautiful alternatives are those teachers who have an eternal place in our hearts. The ones who helped us fly, who nurtured the beginnings of our talents, encouraged us through the tough times, because it wasn't all plain sailing, and who bear significant responsibility for the fact we are now teachers too. You don't have to sit down and consciously make a list of those teachers; you can rattle their names off automatically. You will all have your own Ruby Haynes or Linda Dalglish from primary school; your own Len Clark, Pete Rayman, Bob Brunsden or Stan Bissinger from secondary school.

We have the power to make children feel safe or feel scared, feel loved or feel rejected, purely by how we behave in front of the young, impressionable, people in our classrooms.

Perhaps we forget how some young people idolise the adults they work with in school. My wife teaches in the Early Years and when 3-year-olds from her class see her outside of school the frisson of excitement and fascination is lovely to see. As I write this it is the summer break and one of her class has just turned up at our door with her big sister to give my wife a card that she made. Only recently one of our parents called to let us know that her daughter had created a shrine (her actual word) in her bedroom to the teaching assistant she worked with regularly. Karen, the TA in question, is an exceptional person so she does deserve a shrine, but probably in a more prominent public place. It did make us reflect on a dependency that we needed to watch out for, but the fact remains that our influence is huge and we should be alert to the fact that children may place far more emphasis on some of the off-the-cuff remarks we say or the incidental things we do, both positive and negative, than we do. Take Mrs Burt, for example, who taught me in secondary school. My name clearly amused her, so when she took to reading the register out at the beginning of one lesson she repeated my name, growling the 'ar' in Jarlath a little longer each time. So, Jarlath became, eventually, Jaaaaaaarrrrrrrlath (think pirates, for pity's sake), much to the amusement of my classmates and her. As a grown man I blush very easily. As a 12-year-old boy at secondary school in front of 20 or so classmates I wanted to run away, but I just sat there and took it, going progressively redder with each iteration of the joke, which is precisely why, unforgivably, she carried it on for so long. She won't have given that moment a second's further thought in her life (perhaps she did it to lots of kids), but I will never forget it and it made me very wary of her for the next three years until I could, sadly, drop art forever.

Killer throwaway comments can happen to adults too. 'Oh, you're back! We didn't think you'd make it,' was the first thing that my PGCE tutor said to me as I returned to her school for my second placement there at the end of my teacher training!

Amber

We can turn a child off a subject or off schools and education entirely by our actions, just like Mrs Burt above, but we also have the irresistible potential to be the people who change things for the better for a child who has written themselves off as a failure or who has felt the ice-cold hand of rejection. As I write this, my colleagues and I have just come to the emotional end of two years working with a girl who came to us at the start of Year 10 from another special school. Amber had been at a mainstream primary school and went to a special school for her secondary education due to her combination of learning and behavioural difficulties. Amongst other things, Amber started to walk out of lessons regularly and this escalated to her leaving the school site completely. The school, sited on a main road, took the decision, wrongly in my opinion, that once Amber was off-site she was no longer their responsibility. Amber's mother was so concerned that she removed her from the school and Amber was at home for a whole term before coming to us. It would be disingenuous of me to suggest that all was smooth during Amber's time with us (it wasn't), but she made great progress in regulating her wildly fluctuating emotions and behaviour. Because of her previous experiences Amber was utterly convinced that schools were unsafe places to be, filled with adults who, in her words, 'don't understand me, don't listen to me and don't give a shit about me'. Of course, her previous school will have been full of adults who understood children, listened to them and cared about them. However, in her particular case, she felt a failure and unsafe as she struggled to control her behaviour there at times and, when she needed them most (i.e. when she ran away), she felt they showed disinterest by washing their hands of her. We can argue about the difference between her perception of the situation and that of the adults and the relative merits of both, but a child's perception of you and the climate in your classroom is incredibly important and should not be dismissed. When Amber joined us her finely tuned radar categorised all adults in our school as THREAT. Raised voices, looks of disappointment, assemblies, work that looked too hard and more were all reasons to flee. We needed to explicitly demonstrate to Amber in as many ways as possible, and as often as possible, that we were safe people to be around, that we could be trusted, that we were interested in her and understood her, liked her and cared for her and wanted her to be successful. We needed Amber's guard to drop and for her to feel able to let herself be vulnerable once more. More importantly, at those precise times when she fully expected rejection to rear its ugly head again when things didn't go well, we needed to explicitly demonstrate to her that we would support her and help her to repair relationships and that we would welcome her back the next day with a smile and a redoubling of our commitment to making things better for her.

Of course, none of that is easy. Teachers are human beings too with fluctuating levels of patience and energy, and that is where a supportive team pays off. My colleagues were great at supporting each other and recognising when a change of face was needed (see more on this in Chapter 9 on working in partnership with support staff).

When a child is in such a place as the one Amber found herself in they can resort to the failure avoidance that we discussed in Chapter 1; that is to say, they give up before they even try. Far better to avoid failure than to go through the pain of giving something a go and then have to be told that it (and when they hear 'it' they think 'me') wasn't good enough. When you are convinced rejection will arrive sooner or later the stress of waiting for the inevitable finds an obvious solution – take control by going out on your own terms at a time of your choosing. Be on the lookout for this if you're working with a child who responds with 'I'm not doing it!', rips the work up, refuses to come in to the lesson in the first place, runs out of your lesson, fails to bring their PE kit or regularly complains of feeling ill when the spelling test comes up. These are all potential signs of failure avoidance and your response to this is the single biggest factor in breaking this avoidance cycle.

A significant challenge when working with Amber lay within ourselves. It was the challenge of beating down the negative thoughts when they arose, which they did occasionally – we're human beings remember. In my head these thoughts flitted between thinking that things were getting worse, that colleagues felt that Amber should be excluded by me, that I might cave in to demands to punish Amber more to 'make her behave' and that I was coming across as weak. (Notice how self-centred those thoughts are.) I kept having to remind myself what we were trying to achieve, to remember the progress that had been made so far, and to internalise these thoughts to ensure that Amber didn't see when I was wobbling because that would have unsettled her by suggesting that the rejection she was still expecting was just around the corner.

Remembering those times and the undoubted progress that she did make in the two short years she was with us remind me that we shouldn't mistake kind and humane behaviours from teachers as being soft and permissive, or as letting kids get away with it. You can be both kind and humane whilst also being unwaveringly firm and demanding high standards (a definition of kindness in my view) and it is your actions and your behaviour that will demonstrate this to the children.

In Amber's last week in our school, her last week ever in any school too, we were inspected by Ofsted. On the Tuesday lunchtime Amber and I happened to be walking out of the main building on to the playground when the inspection team were walking the opposite way towards us. 'Are they the inspectors, sir?' Amber enquired. 'Yep,' I replied, wondering what Amber was thinking. 'Can I say something to them?' she said next. 'Er, sure,' I replied, intrigued. Amber, in common with some other Year 11s, had had a couple of rocky weeks brought on by the nervousness leading up to leaving school, so I wondered where this was going.

'Hi! I just want to let you know that this school is much better than my last. I feel safe here. My last school didn't look after me, but the teachers here look after me and they understand me and I feel like I'm getting somewhere with my life.' I had to say to the lead inspector that it sounded positively staged and scripted, but that Amber had just come out with it. We already knew that she felt that way, but it was a heartening moment to see her make the conscious decision to approach three intimidating strangers and say that to them.

There are many facets to our own behaviour, so it is worth taking a closer look at the main ones.

First, do no harm

However we behave as adults working with children, our first job, when deciding how best to deal with behavioural issues, is to ensure we don't escalate the situation, a teacher version of Hippocrates' 'First, do no harm'. There is more to this statement than a consideration of our deliberate actions. We must also give thought to our own emotional state and our reserves of energy and patience. I have been working as a teacher long enough to know when my own capacity to cope runs out. Most of the time I feel as though I have a very significant capacity to work in the most challenging situations with children, but I know that there are rare times when my own emotions get the better of me. These can occur when I have had to deal with difficult situations with colleagues. If I have had a difficult meeting with a colleague, perhaps over their performance, I know that the stress of that remains for a period of time afterwards and my decision-making and tolerance may be compromised (interestingly, difficult meetings with parents or governors, whilst still stressful, do not seem to compromise my resilience in the same way). I am more likely to make poor choices, act too swiftly and say things I will later regret. I know for sure at those times that I need the support of my colleagues and I am not too precious to ask for it. Despite my best efforts, I may escalate a situation and no one benefits from that. To paraphrase Spinoza, people at the mercy of their emotions are not their own master but are instead subject to fortune.

REFLECTION POINTS

- Do you recognise in yourself the times when your capacity to cope with poor behaviour runs out?
- Can you identify the cause(s)?
  - Does fatigue affect you in this way?
  - Does a particular type of behaviour (bullying, for example) affect you in this way?
  - Do issues outside of the classroom, such as workload, or issues outside of school, affect you in this way?
- Where are your sources of support when this happens?
  - Can you call on your support staff?
  - Are the teachers nearby available to help?

Courtesy is contagious

I was on the New York City subway with my family in the Easter of 2017 when a public service announcement came over the tannoy, ending with 'Remember, ladies and gentlemen, courtesy is contagious.' This sums up beautifully the importance of modelling the behaviour we want from our children. They arrive in our classrooms at different stages in their cognitive and emotional development – the spiky profile I mentioned in Chapter 1 – and some basics that we may take for granted will not be automatic for many children, but we can and must show them the way. Welcoming on arrival, a farewell on dismissal, please, thank you, concern for their welfare, showing an interest in their weekend, their hobbies and clubs all contribute to a climate of courtesy and mutual respect that becomes the norm. Sinéad, a diminutive, quiet teacher I worked with in the school for children with behavioural difficulties, had the most impeccable manners and they never, ever slipped, no matter the situation (and some hairy things happened in that school, but she always emerged serene with not a hair out of place). She knew that the only way to develop the same manners in the children we worked with was to relentlessly show them the right way, and because the children respected her enormously, they responded in kind. A colleague of my wife learned this the hard way from a child after being asked for a ruler, to which the teacher demanded, 'Say the magic word.'

'Give me the fucking ruler,' came straight back.

Some interesting relatively recent research by Porath and Erez[1] has looked at how rudeness can affect the people and the culture of the organisations within which we work. In summary, they find that performance, both in terms of cognitive and creative tasks, suffers, but also, and this is really interesting, people also become less helpful to others as a result. It gets worse, as they find that witnesses are affected in similar ways. They also find that a lack of civility leads to dysfunctional behaviour and aggressive thoughts in others. This is how the culture in a classroom or in a school can deteriorate. Let's remind ourselves, though, that we include adults' behaviour in this too. The researchers found that acts of rudeness delivered by an authority figure had the same result. The researchers note that 'When individuals do not feel respected, they tend to either shut down or use up valuable cognitive assets trying to make sense of the environment. Whether they are considering responses, trying to 'explain away' the rude behaviour, or just ruminating about the perpetrator behaviour, it is clear that these processes rob cognitive resources from the task at hand. Incivility drains emotional and cognitive resources necessary for learning and performance.'

Presence

For the first five years of my teaching life I worked in a comprehensive school, neatly split in half by a year in an independent selective school. I felt on top of behaviour for the most part; I knew that high standards that were well understood by the children, communicating well with them, both generally and in terms of the scientific concepts I was teaching them and the good relationships I built, and the creation of a good learning environment were central to that. But I was also sure that I had presence in the classroom – that mysterious quality that the best teachers I aspire to be like have that seems innate, but most certainly is not. By presence I do not mean the emanation of power and control that can scare children – the kind of classroom where nobody dare breathe for fear of facing the wrath of the teacher (think Mr Bronson from *Grange Hill* or Mr Gryce from *Kes* if you're old enough). That kind of presence is damaging as it limits what can be achieved in your classroom because many, if not all, of the children are focused primarily on avoiding getting into trouble and staying invisible. What bothers me, with hindsight, is that as a student teacher I was seduced into thinking that the projection of power was a good thing as it meant I was showing the kids who was boss. I can see now that it was really a projection of my own insecurity as a novice teacher. I was naïvely sure that my six-foot stature and my powerful voice contributed to that, but I was to find soon after, when I left the comprehensive to work in a school exclusively for children with behaviour difficulties, that neither my height nor the power of my voice helped foster good behaviour amongst the children for whom schools were very difficult places in which to feel successful. All the children were in this school because of their significant behavioural issues and most had been permanently excluded from at least one school. It was here that I was able to elicit from my great colleagues, both teachers and support staff, just what this strange aura that is 'presence' actually amounted to. The central point in the entire discussion around presence is not actually whether teachers have presence or not (very few have little); it was what their presence communicated to the children in that classroom. Some bad things happened in our school – the children could be violent towards each other and occasionally towards us, were often verbally very aggressive and situations could escalate extremely quickly. I had to learn fast and all of the staff there were superb in teaching me in the early days. I spent time watching all of them, and over time I managed to tease out a number of deliberate things that they all did that established their presence in the classroom and around the school.

My colleagues had a quiet, inner confidence that conveyed to everyone around them that they were unflappable. No matter the situation it remained outwardly clear to everyone that they took everything in their stride. It was another of the similarities with police officers, and doctors, nurses and paramedics for that matter – their brain might be working overtime, their stomach doing somersaults and their adrenaline racing, yet they exuded confidence and calmness. This was important as it provided great reassurance to the children, both those who were struggling at particular times and the other children around them in the same class.

The children could see that my colleagues were on top of everything. That didn't mean that they needed to be *in control* of everything, that kind of micromanagement is stifling, but it meant that the children knew that the staff would spot anything that fell below their very clear minimum expectations and would deal with it. Further, the children knew how it would be dealt with. There was no nervousness about the unpredictability of the staff. Their consistency was well established.

Most importantly for me, these teachers, all of whom had made the conscious decision to work with children who found schools extremely difficult places to be successful in and could behave extremely violently, communicated to them that they cared. The way they planned their lessons, the ways they spotted when things went well (including communicating with home regularly), the ways they encouraged and supported the children all wrapped up to create a safe place with a sense of security. And, yes, this meant dealing with things firmly, fairly and restoratively when things didn't go well.

REFLECTION POINT

- What does your presence in the classroom communicate about you to the children?

Voice

Our voice is the tool we are most reliant on as teachers. Ever lost your voice? Teaching without it is nigh on impossible. A throat infection will pass, but I only really appreciated how reliant I am on my voice when I first taught children with profound and multiple learning difficulties. If you're working with a child who has multi-sensory impairment, that is to say that they are both deaf and blind, your voice is redundant. They can neither hear you, nor can they lip-read. That is a challenge that few teachers will ever face, although I do think it is something that student teachers should try as it undoubtedly made me a better teacher. I didn't experience that until later in my teaching life, so I didn't appreciate early enough the power of my voice in the classroom.

I was a bit of a shouter when I first started teaching. I worked with some classes where I found it difficult to maintain good order and I resorted to shouting, lazily, because I could (I have a big voice), but mostly because I didn't know what else to do. It shocked most of the children into temporary silence so I deduced that it was effective, although I knew it was something that I should stop.

After some reflection I remembered a teacher of mine from secondary school, Mr Horgan. He was a diminutive man with a husky voice that you had to strain to hear. Our school was lively ('wild' as my former science teacher and Sixth Form tutor said to me recently) so his voice didn't really stand a chance in our classes if he tried to be heard above everyone else. He simply raised his right little finger and waited for us all to do the same. This was our signal to copy him, to be silent and to listen to him. When he first joined the school I wasn't taught by him, but word went round our year group swiftly that this new teacher would hilariously stand at the front of a class of teenagers with his little finger in the air. I remember at the time thinking that it was teacher suicide. But, as above, Mr Horgan had the right kind of presence. He was unflappable and knew that children would respond in time. I realised that shouting indicated a loss of control on my part and that I needed to pay more attention to the after-effects of it on my children and on me so I stopped shouting at my classes, but didn't copy the little finger signal. With one of the classes, a very lively Year 9 science group, we worked up a system whereby I would sit at the back of the class ready for the lesson to start when they arrived. They knew to come in, get their books and pencil cases out on their desks, read anything that was on the board ('Hand your homework in to the tray on my desk', for example) and then come and join me at the back of the lab, round a table on which would be some experiment they would be doing later. It worked beautifully. I didn't have to say a thing – the routine worked really well. They were keen to get started; they knew what they needed to do, so they did it. It was at odds with most of my classes where I would be waiting to welcome them at the door, but I could do that individually as they arrived at the back of the room and I could thank them for the way they started the lesson. With most classes I made sure the lesson started as soon as they sat down. They knew that there would be something on the board or on their desk for them to do and this ensured attention was devoted to work from the off. This reduced the dead time I used to experience if and when children arrived over a five minute period at the start of a lesson.

Meeting our own needs

Whenever I have discussed behaviour with teachers the most controversial topic seems to be when I suggest that we sometimes do things to meet our own needs as adults. We like to think we're pure altruists and that everything we do in school is solely for the benefit of the children in front of us, but sometimes, just sometimes, it's our own needs we're meeting, consciously or otherwise. I will say more about this in Chapter 6 on sanctions and punishments because that is where I see it most often, but it deserves a short mention here because we can escalate situations when there is no need.

Do you ever insist on eye contact? I'm not talking about the rule in a few schools where they insist that all children track the teacher at all times, presumably as some proxy for attention. I'm talking about insisting that a child hold your gaze whilst you're talking to them, maybe because you think they're listening better if they do that, or because you want to impress upon them the seriousness of the discussion. It can be very intimidating for some children to do this and can unnecessarily increase the tension or stress of a situation.

We do something similar when we prolong a situation if we think a child hasn't said sorry properly. 'Now say it like you mean it!' indicates that we won't let it rest until we feel that the child has indicated sincere remorse, even though our way of dealing with it seems unlikely to achieve that and that we can't truly tell if they're sufficiently remorseful anyway. It seems more likely to me to have the opposite effect.

If you want to win that means the child has to lose and this is what I mean when I talk about meeting the needs of adults. The children we work with are probably not too keen on losing, especially in public, and any desire to win or avoid humiliation only really serves to prolong situations. Our relationship with the children we teach is not a zero-sum game so we should ensure we don't create situations where it can be perceived as such by the children.

As the late Joe Bower said,

> When an adult and a child enter into a conversation, the disparity in age by definition creates an imbalance of power. Despite conventional wisdom, this is not the time to increase your adult power; on the contrary, I've found it quite necessary to reduce my adult power and ensure that the child feels like I am not trying to enter into a power struggle by imposing my will on them.
>
> Adults are great at unilaterally imposing solutions in search of a problem and not so great at remembering that there are two problems that need a solution that is mutually satisfactory and durable.[2]

TAKING IT FURTHER – QUESTIONS AND ACTIVITIES FOR YOU AND YOUR COLLEAGUES

- Does our Staff Code of Conduct acknowledge how adult behaviours influence the behaviour of children or is it devoted to dress codes and punctuality? Does it need updating to reflect that?

- In our staff induction is there a section on the behaviour of adults? If not, what do we need to include to ensure it's covered?

- Do we explicitly communicate to children in some way that there is a fresh start after a situation?

- For children who find school a difficult place to be successful, how do we communicate to them that our school is a safe and welcoming place to be? How do we show them that we are adults that can be trusted?

References

1   Porath, C.L. and Erez, A. (2010) 'Are the effects of rudeness real? Can incivility lead to a spiral of aggression and tarnish a culture?' *The Psychologist* 24: 508–511.
2   *Solving Problems Collaboratively: The Ross Greene Approach.* http://joe-bower. blogspot.co.uk/2012/04/collaborative-problem-solving.html (accessed 11 December 2017).

4

RULES AND EXPECTATIONS

The standard you walk past is the standard you accept.

General David Hurley, former Chief
of the Australian Defence Force

THE HEADLINES

- Rules and expectations need to be underpinned by a clear set of values.

- Rules and expectations should enable the creation of a learning environment that is safe and free from disruption.

- Rules and expectations that do not do this are likely to be unnecessary and may actually get in the way by creating conflict where there need be none.

- Actions in response to poor behaviour that are consistent with your values are more effective than consistency of action (i.e. doing the same thing each time, irrespective of circumstances). Treating children equitably is more effective than treating children equally.

- What we allow, what we stop, what we reinforce and what we ignore communicates far more to children than a written set of rules.

- 'Do ...' rules and expectations are more effective than 'Don't ...' rules and expectations. A list of 'Don'ts ...' is inevitably incomplete.

- Make a list of rules and expectations that is short, simple and memorable.

- Ensure reports focus on what a child needs to do to improve.

- Ensure reports are backed up with support for the child to help them achieve that improvement.

- Seating plans can be effective, but only when careful consideration has been given to their construction.

In every single one of the five years I worked in a comprehensive school I was asked by my Head of Year to do the same thing with my tutor group in our first session in September. This thing was a lesson where my tutor group came up with their own set of class rules. Even as an inexperienced teacher I knew that what we were doing was a complete waste of time and I suspect that the children did too. What gave the game away to start with was that we were told how many rules we were to come up with. Five. No more. No less. That's a good start. We were even given a prepared sheet to write them on, complete with the desert island background because everyone knows the best way for children to come up with a set of their own class rules is to get them to imagine being stranded on a desert island. Luckily we did this before the children had the chance to study *Lord of the Flies*. It was a pointless exercise for at least two reasons: the children were heavily influenced by what they thought teachers wanted to hear, so you'd get rules like 'Keep your blazer on at all times', and we all knew that the rules they did come up with couldn't be guaranteed in any other classroom in this big secondary school. We were also only given one hour for 30 children to settle the issue democratically. Even if I taught those children all week long, like many do in primary schools, it would still have been a waste of time because it was done without any discussion or agreement on the values that underpin rules. This is often overlooked and without the necessary values this results in arbitrary or superficial rules that are more to do with obedience as opposed to enabling the values of your class or school to come alive. If you're going to go down the road of children formulating your rules then do it across your entire school underpinned by clear values and do it properly like The Spinney in Cambridgeshire,[1] who have decided that '*Taking care of ourselves, each other, our learning, our school, community and world, and our future*' is the way to go. Otherwise, steer well clear as you are simply pretending and it's an empty exercise, which is a waste of everyone's time and the very definition of inconsistency.

Reinforcing values

Rules that exist without being informed by your values and those of the school run the risk of contradicting what you want your classroom to be about. If you value inclusion and diversity then it makes no sense to rigidly enforce rules without reference to the needs of the children involved. This is the difference between the consistency of action and action that is consistent with your values. The unyielding policy that says that all children will stand when the Headteacher walks into the classroom comes up short when one child is a wheelchair user and cannot stand unaided. Of course you would make an exception in that case, right? Schools that insist that children track the teacher with their gaze would, I hope, make an exception for children such as my daughter with certain visual impairments. Again, an easy adjustment for schools to make, just like the accommodation you would undoubtedly make for a child with a tracheostomy so that they don't have to have their top button done up. Physical difficulties can be accommodated because everyone, children included, can see the obvious reasons for the need to treat these children differently and that those reasons are not the fault of the child. Would you be so accommodating to needs that are less visible? Would you be prepared to let one of your children wear tracksuit bottoms because their significant sensory sensitivity meant that wearing your school trousers was so challenging that it made maintaining concentration very difficult? Are schools more likely to regard this as a child just choosing not to follow the school rules? There is a test to pass here. Do you value inclusion and diversity and, as a result, make reasonable adjustments to ensure the needs of your children are well met and that they don't find themselves in trouble inadvertently or do you value more highly everyone looking the same? Bizarre as this may sound to you, we once allowed a child to wear little beanbags on his shoulders. His mum sewed them on to his polo shirts because they provided the sensory feedback he was craving and were calming for him. They were not disruptive to his learning (quite the opposite) or to anyone else, so the only hurdle to get over was that of the adults accepting how it looked. So? We're in a sorry state if our obsession with uniform can't cope with situations like that. This is not advocating a free-for-all. Actions that are consistent with the values of your school are almost inevitably going to result in treating children differently, that is to say treating them equitably, but not necessarily equally.

In this way you are more likely to develop a learning environment that fosters success and progress from wherever the child is at as opposed to one that simply aims for obedience and is deliberately blind to the differing needs of the children in your care. These classrooms and schools are seen as safe spaces by children where struggle, failure, challenge and difficulties are met with guaranteed support and encouragement.

REFLECTION POINTS

- What values are important to your school?
- What rules does your school have?
- Are your rules aligned with your values?

One fly in the ointment with treating children differently whilst remaining consistent with your values is the perceived injustice that other children can sometimes feel when this happens. Amber, who we met in Chapter 3, was subject to this from some of her peers. I remember having a good discussion with a very outspoken girl in Year 11 who really struggled with the very obvious way that we treated Amber differently. 'Why does she get away with everything?' I was pointedly asked in the playground one day. As a teacher and Headteacher I have always been open to discussing with children why we set the rules we do and we had a really interesting conversation. I tried, in vain I think, to explain to her why, in our special school, we treated all the children differently given their vast range of complex needs. We should be prepared to talk to children about the reasons behind our rules; it is not enough to simply demand blind obedience, especially to rules that may seem at first glance to be silly. We're not giving ground to children or appearing weak if we set out to explain our position to children. Quite the opposite – if we can't explain in simple terms to a child why a rule exists it brings into question the need for the rule to be there at all. Remember the 'No running in the playground' rule from the Introduction I inherited when I first became a Headteacher? I knew it was ridiculous and couldn't defend it to anyone. It was also a prime example of a rule that is unenforceable. Children could find themselves on the wrong side of the school law simply by enjoying themselves, having fun, staying fit and healthy and without doing anything to harm anyone else. If the rule was put in place because play times were rough and boisterous affairs with children being hurt then there are many ways to improve them, but banning running is not one of them.

REFLECTION POINTS

- Can you explain the rationale for the existence of your rules to the children in your class?
- What problems are those rules trying to solve or prevent?

Where do you draw the line?

I must have heard General David Hurley's quote at the start of this chapter, or a version of it, somewhere in my dim and distant past. It has undoubtedly had a subliminal influence on the leader in me as I must sound like a broken record to the colleagues I work with when I regularly come out with 'If you walk past it, you condone it.' This applies equally to teachers in their own classes as it does to the leaders, for whom I am sure General Hurley's advice was originally intended. A written set of rules and expectations is one thing, a vital one for sure, but we must bring this to life by our responses to poor behaviour. We teach children how to behave by what we decide to allow, what we decide to stop, what we decide to reinforce and what we decide to ignore. All of the children in any school are subjected to the same set of expectations, but they know full well through experience what is tacitly allowed or prohibited with each of their teachers in different classes. They have worked out which teacher will continually ask them to put their phone away, but will avoid what they perceive to be confrontation by never enforcing the rule that mobile phones that are seen in school will be confiscated. Similarly, they know which teachers will enforce the rule each and every time. Worst of all, they soon figure out the teachers who are benevolent one day, seemingly overlooking much that goes on, but lurch to zero tolerance the next day when their patience runs out.

Your actions create that all-important sense of security for the children in your classes. They can expect and they deserve fair, predictable responses and there is a difference between this and the blind consistency mentioned earlier. This sense of safety and security is especially important for those who are used to lax or porous boundaries outside of school. You must, though, draw the line in the right place. If your boundaries are too restrictive this can lead to frustration and unrest amongst the children. They can find themselves in trouble for breaking rules that have nothing to do with maintaining a learning environment that is safe and free from disruption. One example I learned of recently was a school that allowed children to wear either long-sleeved or short-sleeved shirts. Fine. However, the children would find themselves in trouble if they had the temerity to roll up their long sleeves. This is a rule that has no place in a school. It exists because we mistakenly equate standards of dress amongst our children with high academic standards (how the University of Oxford copes I have no idea). Surely we can cope with sleeves that look different? By rules such as this we can create conflict and disruption where there would have been none. Unfortunately this uniform highway down which we are travelling is one-way, as to perform a U-turn on expectations of uniform would be seen by many as an erosion of standards. Each year brings new uniform restrictions – all students must have the same school rucksack (what a nightmare for lost property); blazers now have piping on them; trousers and skirts must now have the school logo on them; you will be in detention if the back of your beret is lower on your head than the front (seriously). My brother-in-law, an Irish Guardsman, has turned out in front of the Queen for Trooping the Colour looking shabbier.

What you decide to allow, stop, reinforce and ignore should be targeted towards the creation and maintenance of a safe and supportive learning environment where you can teach and children can learn free from disruption.

Do you have any rules that fall outside of those aims? Ask yourself the following question and then decide if that rule is worth maintaining – what problem or problems is this rule in place to prevent or solve?

I am amazed that the rule that children stand up when the Headteacher, or any adult in some schools, come into a room is still in place today. I have had some interesting discussions with colleagues recently who support this rule and their view is that it shows respect for the Headteacher or adults in general. I struggle to understand how it shows respect because it is mandatory and a child will be in trouble if they don't do it. I think it says more about power than it does about respect or learning. Indeed, it must disrupt learning, even for a short time, every time it happens. Imagine a child trying to read a thermometer every 30 seconds in a physics investigation only to miss one or more measurements, or losing a brilliant last line to a poem that had just come together in their mind because they have to stand up for the Headteacher. The need for deference is such that interruption to learning is regarded as acceptable, but we reserve the right to punish other children if they disrupt learning. This is a clear case of double standards and children can smell that a mile away. I have always thought that the best way a child could show respect to the adults in their school is to work as hard as they can, and to show consideration for their school environment and their peers.

REFLECTION POINTS

- Is low-level disruption a source of frustration for you? If so, do you need to reconsider where you draw the line with:

  - what you allow;
  - what you stop;
  - what you reinforce;
  - and what you ignore?

Dos and don'ts

Rules can either be framed in a positive way as expectations or in a negative way as a list of don'ts. I received some serious criticism when I first became a Headteacher because I boldly said that I didn't believe in rules, I believed in expectations. In hindsight, the message I was trying to convey wasn't communicated very well at all and unnerved some people. What I was trying and failing to say was that a list of don'ts will inevitably be incomplete. Rules and expectations should be explicitly stated in a positive way detailing what you do want rather than what you don't want. *We walk in the corridors* is better than *Don't run in the corridors*. You might think that is mere semantics, but *Don't run* ... allows everything that isn't running, including skipping, doing The Worm or bum shuffling. This explicit statement of what is required as opposed to what is outlawed is also very helpful for some children with special educational needs, as you will see in Chapter 10. You can also help to prevent yourself getting stuck in an argument with a child who has a point when they assert that 'it doesn't say I can't moonwalk down the corridor!'

Making your list of rules and expectations short and simple also helps everyone. Paul Dix advocates *Ready, Respectful, Safe*, for example. This is smart because it is easy for the child (and you) to remember and straightforward for you to refer to when needed. It can also withstand the differences that are inevitably needed for different subjects that are outside, require practical equipment or are in studios such as PE, science or drama, and can equally apply at breaks and lunches. Low-level disruption, the bane of many teachers' lives, can be tackled with reference to the fact that it is not respectful to the rest of the class and the teacher and you cannot be ready for learning either.

Line or sign

The chances are that at some point in your teaching life you have taught someone who is on some form of report for their behaviour. Indeed, if you teach in a secondary school where behaviour is a particular challenge you may have a steady stream of reports to fill in, either in paper form or online, at the end of most of your lessons. Behaviour reports are an interesting beast and a detailed discussion of how to get the best out them and what they should look like belongs in a book on the leadership of behaviour in schools, but they do warrant some mention here.

You may work in a school where reports are standardised – more likely in secondary schools – or you may construct them yourself – more likely in primary schools – but the following points need consideration wherever you work.

Why is the child on report? Reports are always used retrospectively in response to poor behaviour, but sometimes the function of the report is not well thought out. It can be seen as a form of punishment or shame; the public nature of handing a report over to a teacher or the simple act of being placed on report may be considered to encourage the child to sort their life out. I hope you can see that it is both ineffective and has the potential to exacerbate the situation. The report should be clear about the aspect of the child's behaviour that needs to improve and which the report is there to monitor. Being on report in the vain hope it will make the child a better person won't work.

How does it help the child? If the report is simply to punish the child it is singularly unhelpful. If it is constructed in such a way that it helps the child focus on what they need to do to improve then it has some merit. Standardised reports are less likely to be successful in this regard for obvious reasons. I have seen some incredibly helpful, effective and well-constructed reports that help individuals with their own behaviour; they look much like the schedules you will read about in Chapter 10. If the report is there for monitoring reasons only then there is a case for considering why the child should carry it round at all. If it could be done online then this removes the need for the child to simply be the vehicle transporting the report around all day long.

What needs to improve? A report that asks only if the child has behaved well or not is too vague and doomed to failure. These are the kind of reports that are littered with smiley or frowny face emojis on them if a child has been a good or bad person for the last hour. Of course, good or bad is decided by each teacher differently and the child on report can sometimes be held to a different standard than the rest of their classmates. Good reports are explicit in identifying what they are there to monitor – punctuality to lessons, talking when the teacher is talking or the use of foul language, for example. For everything else the child is held to the same standard as the rest of the class without the need to monitor more closely. When I first became a Headteacher our report system was of this nature. It was known as line or sign – a line in the box if behaviour wasn't good enough or signed by the teacher if it was. A line in any box in any one day meant lining up outside the Headteacher's office the next morning. A child could be late to a lesson, say, and receive a line, despite the fact that they were on report for some other reason. They had to see the Headteacher the next morning whereas other latecomers in their class would not.

How long will the child be on report for? Some children seem to be permanently on report. It is legitimate to question the effectiveness of any tactic if nothing is improving (see below regarding support). A review period after every couple of weeks, say, is a good idea. If nothing is changing it would seem futile just to press on without considering what could be done differently.

What support is there behind the report? A report will not change behaviour on its own. It may well help a child to see how they are improving, but the improvement will have come about by the support the adults give the child. If you make a decision to place a child on report, then part of that decision must involve what the adults will do to support the child to improve their behaviour.

Why are you offering a reward? A common theme with reports is the dangling of a reward as an incentive for the child to improve their behaviour. You will read more on my views on rewards in Chapter 5 so I won't go into detail now, but in the next chapter you will learn why I am sure that this aspect of reports is a complete waste of time.

Why are you using the threat of punishment? Less common than rewarding a child for improvement on a report, but still a tactic in use, is the inclusion of a punishment if a child doesn't meet a minimum standard on their report, such as getting more than two frowny faces in a day results in losing their lunchtime the next day. The child is already on report for a particular reason, so this only compounds the issue. The logic behind it seems to be that the threat of further punishment will focus the child's mind on sorting out their behaviour. This is gossamer-thin thinking and adds nothing, or may hinder, attempts to help a child improve their behaviour.

Are you involving parents? Reports can be a way of positively involving parents in attempts to improve their child's behaviour. Many schools now use online systems for monitoring behaviour that allow parents controlled access to their child's information and this can be powerful if designed well. Similarly, reports in paper form can go home each day too, although the chance of them ending up in the bin on the way home is inversely proportional to the success of that day. Well-designed reports also allow parents to start the conversation at home at a productive point. 'What happened during art this afternoon?' is more likely to get to the heart of the matter than 'So, how did today go?'

Reports can, and are, used very well to support children in improving their behaviour, but all too often they are ill-thought out and produced swiftly in a knee-jerk reaction. Careful consideration as to what you are trying to achieve and how you will support the child to get there are cornerstones of a good behaviour report.

Boy, girl, boy, girl; Ladybirds and Dragonflies

Seating plans can be an effective way to foster a positive climate for learning in your classroom when they are constructed carefully. However, when they are put together with no thought as to who the children in front of you are they are likely to be less effective. The rationale for seating plans is that you can help children avoid distracting each other, thereby helping to minimise low-level disruption, by seating those who would choose to sit together away from each other. This rests on the assumption that children will sit with their friends (of course) and this will inevitably lead to disruption, which doesn't automatically follow. My own approach to seating, as I mentioned in the

Introduction, was to give children the responsibility to choose where to sit and to show that they could work having made that choice. I was always explicit with them that I reserved the right to seat them where I wanted without notice. I did move children to a seat of my own choice on occasion, but for the most part it worked well for all concerned.

No seating plan constructed from a class list without first meeting the children will last long. You can inadvertently disadvantage some children if you are not careful, such as those with visual impairments I mentioned earlier – my daughter has to sit near the front because of her eye condition, but has a surname in the second half of the alphabet so would end up nearer the back in an alphabetic set-up. A boy, girl, boy, girl configuration only works if you have equal numbers too and the random nature of such a set-up no more guarantees good behaviour than free choice.

Seating plans are also a means of setting within class and I see this more commonly used in primary schools. This may well be convenient for the teacher and teaching assistant(s) but the children read a lot into the meaning of these groupings. To quote my daughter 'I'm on Ladybirds, but I really want to be on Dragonflies because they do better [interesting word] work than we do,' and to quote my son from when he was in primary school, 'I'm on the second best table for maths'. Children make interesting and sometimes worrying assumptions about themselves, their classmates and their relative importance based on such observations and we must ensure that we don't inadvertently send them messages that some children are less or more important. An unintended consequence of such groupings occurs if and when children move tables. Imagine if my daughter hadn't gone 'up' (as she would have said) to Dragonflies, but instead went 'down' (as she would have seen it) to Grasshoppers? Try convincing her that that wasn't a demotion.

Rules and expectations are there to help create and maintain a great environment for teachers to teach so that children can learn. For that to happen the children must be free from harm or the threat of harm from other children and free from disruption to their limited and very valuable learning time. Anything that does not assist in the creation and maintenance of that environment is an addition to your work that you can do without. Indeed, unnecessary rules can create disruption and conflict where there needn't be any. Situations where children find themselves in trouble for saying 'OK' after being told off (this is an actual school rule that I would inadvertently break all the time given that 'OK' is such an automatic response) or where children are held to higher standards of behaviour expectations than the adults in the school are getting in the way of the learning environment that you want and crave and should be ditched. Keep your rules and your expectations simple, positive and straightforward and you have the best chance of creating the environment you want.

TAKING IT FURTHER – QUESTIONS AND ACTIVITIES FOR YOU AND YOUR COLLEAGUES

- Can the children in our school recite our rules? If not, do they need to be simplified?

- Are our rules humane enough to make reasonable adjustments for children with particular difficulties, such as some special educational needs?

- Do we mandate seating plans? What parameters do we set for teachers when doing this?

- Do our seating plans convey messages to our students about their ability compared to their peers?

- How effective do we consider the report system to be in school? Does it focus on what needs to improve?

Reference

1 'The school that can fit its rules onto one hand', *The Guardian*, 20 October 2011. www.theguardian.com/education/2011/oct/20/school-i-would-like-spinney (accessed 11 December 2017).

5

MOTIVATION AND REWARDS

Children should experience success and failure not as reward and punishment but as information.

Jerome Bruner

THE HEADLINES

- Recognising good behaviour is more effective than rewarding good behaviour.

- Recognising progress is more effective than recognising achievement.

- Ensure that recognition reaches parents swiftly.

- Offering rewards fosters self-interest.

- Offering rewards conveys the message that learning and behaving for their own sake are not worth the effort.

- Public rankings of rewards do far more harm than good.

- Learning needs to be a rewarding experience.

- Learning does not need to be fun or exciting.

- Learning environments and adults need to be regarded by children as safe and secure.

- Intrinsic motivation is more effective in influencing good behaviour than extrinsic motivation.

- Intrinsic motivation (doing something because it is the right thing to do) is characterised by:
  - a thirst for knowledge;
  - a sense of accomplishment;
  - activities that are satisfying in and of themselves.

- Extrinsic motivation (factors that encourage behaviours that are a means to an end and not for their own sake) is characterised by:
  - gaining something (i.e., a reward) or avoiding something (i.e., a punishment);

- o   the existence of a rule or task driving rule-following or task-completing behaviour;
- o   rules or tasks being valued.

- Extrinsic motivation can result in the bare minimum being done in order to secure a reward or to avoid a sanction.

In the preface to Alfie Kohn's (1993) *Punished by Rewards*[1] he tells of a project he carried out at college in which starved, caged rats learned that they would be rewarded with Rice Krispies that would appear every time they pressed a little bar. The account contains a nice twist because Kohn concludes in his project report that the rats 'trained a college student in breakfast-feeding behaviour'. Amusing, yes, but Kohn uses it to make a very powerful point; that we are in love with pop behaviourism. That is to say, we are in love with the notion that good behaviour is achieved by deploying the 'Do this and you'll get that' technique. We are so in love with it that it has become our default go-to tactic when trying to encourage good behaviour or improve poor behaviour yet we fail to see how limiting it is and that, at its heart, is the world-view that the best way to motivate people to do things is to offer a reward without which their motivation would plummet and they would be far less likely to complete the task at hand. The use of rewards characterises misbehaviour simply as a matter of motivation – the child is always regarded as making a premeditated choice (that word again) to misbehave and can be incentivised to comply. It has everything to do with doing and nothing to do with learning. *'Do this, get that'* is not the same as *'Do this, learn that'*. You may argue that in order to learn the child must first do what the teacher had planned, but this 'carrot and stick' approach simply fosters self-interest. We reach for it every time we put a child on report – there is a box at the bottom of the report card that dangles a reward in front of the child if they get enough ticks, gold stars or smiley faces at the end of the day or week. There is a reason it's the first thing we reach for. If we're honest we all know that one of the reasons we resort to rewards is because they are simple and easy to implement – just think of something enticing, dangle it in front of the child and expect an improvement in behaviour. It requires little thought on our part, but crucially, and this is its Achilles heel, it requires nothing from us beyond providing the reward. We don't have to change or do things differently and this is why it is ineffective in providing behaviour change. Kohn goes to town over the course of 300-plus pages on rewards in all their forms and I won't rehearse his arguments here. You can read them for yourself and decide if children really are punished by rewards, but I will take up the baton about our understanding of motivation, the use of rewards and how little thought we give to the thinking behind their deployment and the negative, non-existent or, at best, short-term superficial effects of their use.

In this chapter I am going to ask you to think hard about the motivation of the children you teach and of how you use rewards in your daily work – effort stickers and their public display on your classroom wall, Vivo points, handwriting pens and the like. I am going to get you to think about intrinsic motivation – doing something for its own sake because it is the right thing to do or because it is satisfying – and extrinsic motivation – doing something only in return for a reward or to avoid a sanction or punishment (more on that in Chapter 6). It is my view that it is the recognition that children receive, the information contained therein, as Bruner would say, that has the transformative effect, not the reward dangled in front of them. It is not grandiose public recognition either. That is done normally by teachers on the basis that they think that by publicly praising one child this will incentivise others to do the same – it probably won't. Further, the reward shifts attention away from the recognition, negating its effect (see the section below on comparisons with grades and comments in feedback). I will also want you to think about who is, dare I say it, over-represented in your current rewards systems. I suspect that there will be two groups: the children who are achieving highly academically and for whom behaviour is never, and would probably never be, an issue under any system; and the children whose behaviour you are working hardest to improve and whom you are most likely to try to encourage to behave well by pouncing on the merest hint of compliance or cooperation.

It is my position that any system to support positive behaviour in your class must recognise progress too. In fact, I will go further – recognising progress is *more* important than recognising achievement. Every August local and national newspapers in England have front page photographs of lines of teenagers in a badly choreographed leap clutching sheaves of papers with, no doubt, strings of A* and A grades. My thoughts always turn to the children who overcame significant learning difficulties, studied incredibly hard and were proud of their grades which, by comparison, may have seemed poor to others. Patrick, mentioned in Chapter 1, earned two Fs at GCSE (in maths and science) and these were tremendous achievements for him given his deep-seated literacy and behavioural difficulties. In our school we were able to celebrate those for what they were – recognition that a young person had come a long way in a short time. He had changed from someone who rejected schools and those in them with aggression and abuse and was firmly of the view that schools were unsafe and unrewarding places to be into someone who could once again feel successful in school. Which is worthy of greater recognition – 12 A*s or two Fs? Of course we will all say that it depends on the context, but I fear that almost all rewards systems out there are blind to this. It is common in behaviour training offered to teachers to hear the mantra 'Catch them being good' when what you really need to do is catch them being better.

REFLECTION POINTS

Take a look at your school or class reward system and reflect on how it actually works. Ask yourself:

- Why are we giving out rewards?

- What would happen if we simply stopped giving out rewards tomorrow?

- Would the children notice?

- Would it *really* matter to them?

- Would the quality of their work be affected by the cessation of rewards?

- Would their behaviour deteriorate in the absence of rewards?

- What are we *actually* rewarding when we give out rewards?

- Do children sometimes receive rewards without realising what they are for?

- Do some of our children think that they have no chance of a reward in our system?

- Do we reward progress or do we reward high achievement?

- Are we noticing some children more than others?

Do you need to make some changes as a result?

I am in the fortunate position of being able to visit lots of schools. Much of the time I am visiting because we have been asked to consider a child for admission to our school. Occasionally these visits are to secondary schools where a child's place may be at risk of breaking down, typically because the behaviour of the child has become something the school is no longer prepared to accept, and we are being considered as a more suitable school. I spent the afternoon at a secondary school recently in a lesson with a Year 9 class. The teacher walked in (after the children by the way) and their first words were: 'There will be a bunch of points in it for you all if you can hold it together this afternoon.'

Immediately I shifted in my seat from facing away from the majority of the class to facing towards the entire class out of sheer curiosity as to what was about to unfold. This school, in common with many others, operated a reward system devised by external companies based on points that are awarded to children in schools for things such as behaviour, school work and attendance (imagine being penalised for being ill). These points accumulate and can be redeemed for prizes from the online shop of the company who host their system. You can see that the opening remark from the teacher set the scene for the lesson to follow. He had no expectation that the children would behave well without, frankly, bribing them. He had not even told the class what the lesson was to be about and so had not given the children the chance to decide that the lesson was going to be rubbish or amazing anyway. As it turned out it was one of those lessons where the class repeatedly fill the vacuum caused as soon as the teacher stops talking, and the teacher then has to go through endless rounds of shushing and requesting silence ('I've got my GCSEs, it's your own time you're wasting,' as Hywel Roberts parodies semi-seriously) before continuing with the lesson. (And I didn't see any points being awarded at the end of the lesson, in case you're wondering.) This is the road we walk down with shiny rewards. They may well be worth something in monetary terms, but their value is precisely zero. Their use conveys a clear message, one that the teacher above communicated loud and clear – this work is to be endured; there is no value in completing it for its own sake and to make it worth your while here is something to sugar the pill. And it didn't even work anyway.

Rewards – fostering self-interest

I have three main concerns with rewards. Firstly, they convey the message that learning and behaving for their own sake are not worth the effort. It only becomes worth it in order to gain something in return. Secondly, I worry that rewards breed a selfish mindset. 'What's in it for me?' becomes the question to be answered, the test to be passed before the child buys in to what you have planned. This cannot be right. It rests on an assumption I mentioned in the introduction – the child is fully capable of doing this work or behaving well, they are simply choosing not to so they can be incentivised to comply. If only life were so simple. Thirdly, I have strong suspicions that they are inequitably distributed (and I categorically do not mean 'rewards for all' here). This is a tough place to go without sounding like I am accusing the profession of discrimination. My concern is that we may naturally be inclined to reward an A* achievement for a child who was always on track to get an A*, yet fail to acknowledge the child who achieved an E yet who, based on their prior attainment, was predicted a G. When I taught GCSE science I had a conversation with a senior manager that set me thinking on this path. 'You need to get Guy from his E-grade to a C,' came the demand (C being the magic line to cross). My heart sank because Guy had been predicted an F based on his Key Stage 3 SATs scores. That is not to say that I felt Guy should sit on his laurels, but he did deserve recognition for making solid progress so far. He certainly didn't deserve pressure that made him feel as though he was failing, again. He got his E, which was a tremendous achievement for him, despite what my boss thought.

Be clear about the distinction between a reward and a child receiving recognition for something that they have done. To reiterate the point made at the start of the chapter, it is recognition (Bruner's information), especially recognition of progress and the information passed to the child about their progress, that leads to lasting improvements in behaviour.

Let's take a look at some of the more common rewards that we see used in schools.

Effort stickers – A favourite in primary schools, especially with younger children. Perhaps you use these? Do they do what their name says they do? Do they *really* recognise effort? Or are you recognising attainment or ability, things that are poor proxies for effort, in some roundabout way? Does 10/10 in spelling tests every week really indicate the amount of effort that went in to that? Does it overshadow the child who has moved from 1/10 every week to 3/10? Are you recognising effort, achievement or progress here? To be consistent with my point above you can recognise effort, and effort is something that is certainly worth recognising, but do you really have to display this publicly? The effort sticker chart next to your board is on show all day long and is a public league table of the children in your class. Someone, a child, is at the bottom of that, and they know they're at the bottom as does everyone else in the class.

There is no merit in this whatsoever. Why does it need to be on display? If the thinking goes that those with few stickers will up their game to try to catch up, then try the same in the staffroom with teachers and see how long it lasts. Would you be OK with an effort sticker league table of teachers in your staffroom? How about in your Reception area for the visitors to see? We would rightly argue that this would kill staff morale, yet we merrily do this to children every day. Recognise effort, or anything else that you deem to be valuable for learning, but understand the limitations and drawbacks that are created the second you start displaying totals publicly and turning it into some sort of competition. This will rear its head again in Chapter 6 on sanctions and punishments when we write children's names on the board for misdemeanours or use traffic light behaviour systems.

Points mean prizes – A favourite in secondary schools. Points are awarded for various things such as good behaviour, attendance (a punishment for being ill it seems [see below]), merits or credits awarded, percentage of homework completion and the quality of work completed. I hope the tale above highlights to you how limiting these points systems are and the clear message they send – these things are not worth doing for their own sake. A common response from teachers when I make this point is 'What about the kids who are doing the right thing, day in, day out? Surely they should be rewarded for that?' I reiterate my earlier point – *you need to catch them being better, not reward them for being good.* Think Bruner again – it is the recognition that is important, not the £20 voucher at the end of it.

100% attendance rewards – OK, hands up, I used to do this, but I was asked once by a parent why I was punishing children for being ill and I couldn't answer her. All schools want to encourage the highest possible attendance and there is nothing wrong with that. This just goes too far and identifies not being ill as something to reward someone for. The extension of that being that someone who is unwell is somehow responsible for their ill-health and could have been in school if only they'd had a better attitude. Think who is most disadvantaged by this system – children with leukaemia, children who break their arm representing the school at football, children who catch a virus from another child in school who was a carrier, didn't get ill and got their 100% certificate in assembly. Fair? Hardly.

Handwriting pen licences – These exist in many, many primary schools and are awarded when a teacher judges that a child has achieved a certain level of fluency, speed and legibility with their handwriting and can then move on from writing in pencil to writing in pen. They are a specific example of the least effective extrinsic motivation (see below) and I have never fully understood why these milestones exist as they seem to penalise children with fine motor control problems. It is clearly important for children to write fluently, legibly and at pace, but this can be hampered by, for example, a condition that means they have lax ligaments (surprisingly common) and will, therefore, tire easily and struggle with good posture (the number of key components to good handwriting is surprisingly long and something I knew nothing about until I worked in a special school). The race to achieve the licence was brought home to me when both my son and daughter were in infant school and would regularly tell me that yet another classmate had been awarded their licence and they still hadn't got theirs. I don't get it. Why is writing in pen better than writing in pencil anyway? Some children print as opposed to write cursively too. Fluency, speed and legibility are important, but the medium and style shouldn't carry so much weight.

Time off work for good behaviour – Be very careful with this. Are you conveying the message that work, and therefore learning, is something that gets in the way of free choice and Golden Time? This is how it will come across if most of your class are on the field playing and you have three or four children left behind doing maths. The other side of this particular coin (mentioned again in Chapter 6 on punishments) is to threaten to deny the child access to an element of the curriculum that is perceived to be enjoyable – 'If you don't do this then you can't do swimming.' This is a big no-no as you would be using something that a child is entitled to as a bargaining chip.

Mission impossible – Some reward systems put some children in unwinnable positions. You may be in danger of this if you set arbitrary benchmarks for rewards. Rewards for 100% attendance are just such an example and are known as 'all-or-nothing' situations (remember these from Chapter 2 on psychology?). The danger with arbitrary benchmarks is that some children will cross them with ease and others may feel, genuinely or otherwise, that the reward is unattainable. It is easy to see how your motivation can wane if you judge that you have no chance of earning the reward. A particularly egregious example I encountered was that attendance at the end of Year 11 Prom after GCSEs was conditional on children earning a certain number of points. I can guarantee that the points threshold will be out of reach for some children whilst others will cross it with ease. This is a ham-fisted attempt to motivate some of the children to up their game in their studies, and some will fall short because if they all passed then the threshold will be deemed to be too low. I find it upsetting that a school would make acceptance to an end-of-school celebration conditional in this way. This can only foster resentment. To reiterate my main point in this chapter, it is recognition of progress that counts here. Children inevitably start from different positions, so accounting for that is likely to avoid feelings of injustice which, as all teachers know, children feel very keenly indeed. I know I would if I was prevented from attending a party simply because I struggled with some aspects of school life.

Comparisons with assessment for learning

Paul Black and Dylan Wiliam's seminal work from 1998, *Inside the Black Box*,[2] set the ball rolling in a big way on improving teachers' use of formative assessment, also known as assessment for learning (assessment used to promote children's learning as opposed to summative assessment which is used for certification, such as in exams, or to rank children for setting and grouping or for whole school accountability, such as in Year 6 SATs). Part of the push from that work was the acceptance that the use of grades, marks or percentages 'has a negative effect in that pupils ignore comments when marks are also given' (Butler, 1998[3]). We do not use this to inform our understanding of how to improve behaviour, but we should. The grade, be it an A or a G, is a statement with no advice on how to improve. It is the equivalent of the Vivo points, the bar of chocolate or the Golden Time that takes the attention away from and negates the recognition of the good behaviour. Consider this in light of your feedback to children about their behaviour. *Make the act of feeding back, with Bruner's information contained within, the most powerful and important part of the process.* A clear understanding from the child about what they have done well, what they now need to do to improve and, crucially, how you can help them to succeed once more if they need your support is far more valuable.

Black and Wiliam also assert that 'to be effective, feedback should cause thinking to take place'. You can see that this will also be true for improving behaviour. It is one thing to tell a child that their behaviour is unacceptable and what they need to do to change it, but there is power in helping them to think through the process. This is very much in the spirit of the restorative approaches described in Chapter 7. Leading questions such as 'How can this be put right?', 'Who has been affected by this?' and 'How have they been affected?' can be painful for the children to answer and can be time-consuming for you but are far more effective in the longer term than 'You were wrong. Say sorry. Now. And mean it.'

Lastly, Black et al. conclude that children have to change from 'behaving as passive recipients of the knowledge offered by the teacher to becoming active learners who could take responsibility for, and manage, their own learning' (p.10).[4] To paraphrase, surely we all want schools full of children who are no longer passive recipients of rewards and sanctions for good or poor behaviour offered by the teacher but children who take responsibility for, and manage, their own behaviour because that is the right thing to do.

A chance to involve parents

Recognising good behaviour or improvements in behaviour is vital, but we miss a trick if we don't take the chance to share the good news with parents (there will be more on this in Chapter 8). Know that for some parents the school phone number flashing up on their phone fills them with dread. It means only one thing, 'Can you come and collect your child as their behaviour has been unacceptable this morning'. I work with one family who recount that their experience of middle school was a cycle of the mother dropping Harry off at school and then going home to wait for the phone to ring, which it almost inevitably did every day. Can you imagine living like that? That is why communicating good news to parents is a no-brainer, an easy win. The continuation of a positive conversation from school to home is always a good thing. It buys confidence with the parents and the added bonus is that children know that school and home communicate with each other. Make a phone call, send a postcard home, write a note in the planner, send an e-mail. Whatever works for you and the parents, but ensure that you do it.

A chance to involve colleagues

You read in Chapter 2 about the faulty thinking involved when we ignore positives and focus on negatives. Sharing good news messages with colleagues can help to combat this. This is doubly important in a secondary school, where a child will have a number of different teachers. A narrative can build up around certain children that labels them (also in Chapter 2) as a behaviour problem. *Sharing when things have gone really well, especially for those children for whom school might be the most challenging place to be successful, is extremely important.*

Intrinsic motivation

I have worked for over a decade now in special schools with children with learning difficulties and seen hundreds of them battle day in, day out trying to master things that many children their age can do with no conscious effort, such as writing their name, reciting their number bonds to 100 or tying their shoelaces. I never cease to be impressed that they turn up every day with a positive mental attitude, grit their teeth and give their best. How long would it take for you to give something up? How many setbacks would you cope with before you decided that it wasn't worth the pain and the heartache? As an aside, I always think about children with learning difficulties when I read about the current trends of growth mindset and grit being the route to a string of A* grades – these children are some of the grittiest people I know. Bear in mind too that it is not uncommon for our children to appear to have learned something one day only for it to frustratingly vanish the next day. It would be a fair assumption that these children find this such an intensely exasperating experience that they would simply refuse to carry on after a time. I know I would. The *Teach Yourself German in the Car* CDs that have been in my glove box for four years are testament to that. What is it about these children, the classrooms they are working in, and the teachers they are learning from that mean that they persevere despite the repeated struggles, setbacks and feelings of failure?

First and foremost these classrooms and the people in them are regarded by the child as safe. A child can be intensely interested in any topic you care to name, but if the environment isn't right or if the child perceives there to be a level of threat it is harder to learn. You may never have thought of your classroom, or you for that matter, in this way before. I certainly didn't for my first few years as a teacher. I have worked with many children now, though, who have left other schools because of their behaviour and it is common for them to think this way, to develop a narrative, an internal conversation, along the following lines:

- Teachers and classrooms are unsafe because:
  - I am given work I cannot do.
  - When I cannot do it I am punished.
  - I still can't do the work.
  - Sooner or later you give up on me.

It then becomes safer for them, so their logic goes, to protect themselves by quitting on their own terms. Why wait for inevitable rejection when they can control how and when it happens?

In my experience this lack of a feeling of safety is a major problem for many of the children I've worked with who have found schools difficult places to be successful. As I said in Chapter 1, we work incredibly hard to make sure the children know we're there to catch them, not catch them out. Sometimes this will result in us explicitly saying to a child, 'We're not going to give up on you.' If this sense of security is established, and bear in mind that it is well established for the vast majority of children, then you're in business. As Melanie Cross says in her excellent book *Children with Social, Emotional and Behavioural Difficulties and Communication Problems: There Is Always a Reason*, 'in learning, one is exposing one's own ignorance, which is not possible without feeling secure in the situation where learning occurs' (p.154).[5] In these high-challenge/low-threat environments, as Mary Myatt describes them,[6] children view their work and their learning as satisfying and fulfilling. *For them learning is a rewarding experience.* This sense of satisfaction or fulfilment drives an intrinsic motivation to learn and comes in many different ways:

- **There is a thirst to know** – It can be hard to pin down exactly where this can come from, but we all have topics that fascinate us, sometimes for no apparent reason. My son is currently studying the Second World War and his interest is heightened because of the stories he is hearing about his great-grandfathers. Yesterday he was learning about the Nazi concentration camps in school and then came home to learn that one of his great-grandfathers had helped to clear one of them after the war. As a result it is non-stop questions in our house about this topic – he just can't get enough.
- **There is a sense of accomplishment** – The child feels that they are making steady progress; they are getting somewhere with this topic or subject. This allows them to approach challenges in this subject confident that they have the knowledge and skills to make further progress. A particularly satisfying example of that is when something that was once considered impossible becomes possible. Do you recall the fuzzy feeling in your belly the first time you swam by yourself, rode a bike without stabilisers or calculated the roots of a quadratic equation?

I wonder if as adults we sometimes forget the magical feelings generated by those situations? Daniel Muijs and David Reynolds (2011)[7] note that 'the effect of achievement on self-concept is stronger than the effect of self-concept on achievement'. That is to say that it is achievement that is the driver of motivation, not the other way round. It is not simply a matter of attitude or mindset.

- **The activity is regarded by the child as satisfying in and of itself** – Swimming and other sensory activities are good examples of such. This is likely to be the case only when a level of competence has been achieved – if you simply cannot swim then it is far from satisfying! I hate golf with a passion for this reason. I like many sports and will happily give most a go, knowing that my half-decent hand–eye coordination and fitness will see me through. I am with Mark Twain on golf though. It needs a level of competence that requires time and effort that I don't have. I remember this every time I see children struggle to summon up the motivation to tackle an English or maths problem that they've been working on for what may feel like an eternity.

The work has an intrinsic value to the child and that is the heart of the matter. There is no need for material persuasion to get the job done. It is worth the effort, however difficult (and this is where perseverance appears), for its own sake.

One factor that I have made less of that influences intrinsic motivation is the agency or autonomy of the children. This is because, within school, children have significantly less autonomy than they do outside of school, but it is worth bearing in mind. There is very little true choice for children in our schools, but it's not entirely absent. They may have some choice in, let's say, art but they are likely to be working within a theme dictated by the teacher or the exam board. As a science teacher I can think of very little autonomy that I gave the children I taught. The curriculum was set by someone else, I differentiated accordingly and decided how best to teach my classes. As the children get older we allow an element of choice when we allow them to choose options (or reject options in some cases) at about Year 9. This increases to full choice about subjects at post-16 for A-Level, but the curriculum is still imposed for obvious examination reasons. It is simply worth considering that agency is a factor in intrinsic motivation and there is very little of it available to children within school.

Fun

Learning does not need to be fun or exciting. I see advice provided to teachers that activities should be fun as a way of preventing behavioural issues arising and of increasing motivation. This advice is misguided. Any fun that arises out of learning is a by-product. Don't get me wrong, it is a welcome by-product, but it is neither an aim to be achieved when planning learning, nor is it a necessary outcome of learning. It is advice that leads to attempts to teach topics through the medium of a child's favourite sport, computer game or trading card game – extrinsic motivators and poor ones at that. You should be able to see how difficult life becomes for the teacher who succumbs to this advice; either the whole class has to endure Pokémon arithmetic because the one child you're struggling to engage in maths is obsessed with that, or the teacher has to produce numerous different sets of resources to cater for the different interests of the children. Neither gets you any further down the road to better learning or better behaviour. They are surefire ways, though, to increase your workload, your photocopying and laminating budget and your tiredness.

Extrinsic motivation

Extrinsic motivation amounts to factors that encourage behaviours that are a means to an end and not for their own sake, but it is not simply limited to tangible rewards. There are a number of ways in which people are extrinsically motivated to do something or to behave in a certain way when intrinsic motivators run dry.

- **At the most basic and least effective level behaviour is regulated by an external reward or constraint** – These are the classic 'gain or avoid' situations. I have made much of the 'gain' part of this in the earlier part of this chapter when looking at rewards so I hope you will see how limiting this method of motivation is. The more negative 'avoid' aspect of this is the pressure to behave simply in order to escape something such as a sanction or punishment – the deterrent effect. Much is made of this by teachers – that we should make an example of one child in order to provide a deterrent to others and that the existence of tough rules will deter children from behaving badly in the first place. In all my years of teaching I have never believed this to be true. I am a firm believer that many children are doing the right thing day in, day out because it is the right thing to do. As I said earlier, this form of behavioural pressure has everything to do with compliance and nothing to do with learning. You can see in this case that a child may do the bare minimum to avoid a sanction. They are unlikely to invest everything they have into their work in order to do their best if they are simply seeking to evade a consequence.
- At the level above simple reward or punishment a child may be motivated to go along with a task or follow a rule simply *because* the

task or rule exists and feel guilty if they don't. The presence of rewards or punishments is not important, as it is the self-imposed pressure to conform, complete a task or stick to the rules that provides the incentive to behave. As above though, the point of the activity, the learning involved or the satisfaction to be gained is irrelevant. 'Good students sit in silence in assembly. I want to be a good student, so I will sit silently regardless of what the assembly is about or how mind-numbingly boring it is.' I believe there to be a large amount of this going on with children in schools and it certainly describes almost all of my schooling until 16.

- **Beyond this, once a child begins to see the benefit of a school rule or a task they begin to value it** – The work is moving them closer to a goal they are trying to attain. Examples might be that there is value to a child in securing a maths A-Level in order to become a pilot, obtain a certain set of grades to secure a place at medical school or carry out a daily training programme as they aim for a place in the first XV rugby squad. The attainment of progress applies here too. They may not actually enjoy the subject that much, but know that it is a key to a future aspiration. It has value, but not intrinsic value.

REFLECTION POINTS

Think of a class that you are working with and of something that you are try-ing to work on with them. Perhaps it's the quality of homework and its com-pletion rate? Where do you place the children on this ladder of motivation?

- A sense of satisfaction or enjoyment.
- A sense of accomplishment.
- A thirst to acquire knowledge.

Could their behaviour be influenced by motivation to ...

- achieve a goal or target?
- follow a rule or rules?
- avoid a sanction or gain of a reward?

What could you and your team do to inch them that little bit further away from doing it simply to avoid a sanction and that little bit closer to valuing it for its own sake?

The idea that you could shift the motivation of *all* of your students *all* of the time to the top of that ladder is unrealistic. It is not unrealistic, though, to think about what it will take to shift children from wherever they are on that ladder to a position a bit nearer the top.

You can see that the motivation to avoid a detention, say, or to avoid breaking a rule is extremely limiting and children are unlikely to be putting their heart and soul into their work when the goal is task completion or punishment avoidance and not learning. The realisation by the child that there is some value, intrinsic or otherwise, can help them move away from this motivational trough. Clearly there is likely to be more buy-in and more effort here and as a result the outcome is likely to be better. It should not take much persuasion to allow you to see why we want children to value the work they are doing, and the expectations we have for them as worthwhile and valuable. I hope you can see that the lure of a shiny reward at the end is highly unlikely to persuade a child to develop any deeper kind of motivation to behave better or take a greater interest in their work. To repeat my paraphrasing of Black and Wiliam above, surely we all want schools full of children who are no longer passive recipients of rewards and sanctions for good or poor behaviour offered by the teacher but children who manage and take responsibility for their own behaviour because that is the right thing to do.

TAKING IT FURTHER – QUESTIONS AND ACTIVITIES FOR YOU AND YOUR COLLEAGUES

- Consider having a week completely free of rewards. Focus instead on recognising good behaviour and progress in good behaviour – *catch them being better.* Note what happens during the week and at the end of it. What happened to behaviour? What happened to the quality of the children's work?

- Ask yourselves what are we currently recognising and rewarding in our behaviour policy?

- Why are we recognising and rewarding these things?
  - o Is there a danger we are *really* rewarding something else? (For example, do we award effort stickers to children who achieved the highest grades as opposed to those who actually worked the hardest?)

- What do we really want to recognise? Why do we want to recognise these things?

(Continued)

- Are we publicly displaying reward charts and ranking children? Why are we doing this?

- Do we have arbitrary benchmarks for rewards and recognition that some children meet with ease and others feel are impossible to achieve?

- Are we using a 'carrot and stick' approach to motivation?
  - Look out for rewards and punishments as examples of this – 'do this, get that' or 'do this, avoid that'.

- Can we encourage our children to use better forms of motivation by instilling in them:
  - a thirst for knowledge?
  - a sense of accomplishment and a feeling that they are making progress?

References

1   Kohn, A. (1993) *Punished by Rewards: The Trouble with Gold Stars, Incentive Plans, As, Praise and Other Bribes.* New York: Houghton Mifflin.

2   Black, P.J. and Wiliam, D. (1998) *Inside the Black Box: Raising Standards through Classroom Assessment.* London: King's College.

3   Butler, R. (1998) 'Enhancing and undermining intrinsic motivation: the effects of task-involving and ego-involving evaluation on interest and performance', *British Journal of Educational Psychology,* 58: 1–14.

4   Black, P.J., Harrison, C., Lee, C., Marshall, B. and Wiliam, D. (2002) *Working Inside the Black Box: Assessment for Learning in the Classroom.* London: King's College.

5   Cross, M. (2011) *Children with Social, Emotional and Behavioural Difficulties and Communication Problems: There Is Always a Reason.* London: Jessica Kingsley Publishers.

6   Myatt, M. (2016) *High Challenge, Low Threat: How the Best Leaders Find the Balance.* Woodbridge: John Catt Educational Ltd.

7   Muijs, D. and Reynolds, D. (2011) *Effective Teaching: Evidence and Practice,* 3rd edn. Los Angeles, CA: Sage.

6

SANCTIONS AND
PUNISHMENTS

'The same old faces. 10 years this school's been opened, and for 10 years after every assembly we see a line of boys here, and the same old faces.'

Mr Gryce, *Kes*

THE HEADLINES

- Sanctions and punishments used in schools rely heavily on behaviourist principles – rewarding good behaviour and punishing poor behaviour – and this is why they are generally ineffective in improving behaviour.

- We reach for sanctions and punishments to satisfy the need to do something tough in response to poor behaviour.

- Detentions, one of our most common sanctions, use loss of free time and inconvenience to lead to behaviour change. This dead time could be reduced significantly and could be used more productively if we did restorative work with the children in that time.

- For a sanction to be effective as a deterrent the most important factor is the likelihood of being caught breaking the rule, not the harshness of the sanction itself.

- Deterrents are not factors in serious and stressful situations when people are rarely thinking coolly and rationally.

- Loss aversion, such as the threat of confiscation, may buy you short-term compliance but not behaviour change.

- If the threat of a sanction is the only thing persuading a child to work or behave, you are likely to get only the bare minimum out of them to avoid getting into trouble.

- Work can be regarded as a chore if it is associated with sanctions, such as working when the rest of the class earn free time or when added to detentions to fill dead time.

- Shaming or embarrassing children by, for example, writing their name on the board or using class traffic light systems in order to secure compliance is counter-productive.

- Shaming can escalate situations through a child:
  o withdrawing (by introversion or physical withdrawal);
  o denying or avoiding (by attempting to minimise or deny the experience);
  o turning negative emotions inwards (feeling contempt for themselves and known as *attacking self*);
  o turning negative emotions outwards (known as *attacking others*).

- Preventing access to a part of a child's curriculum entitlement that they enjoy, such as PE, in an attempt to improve behaviour should never be done.

- Sanctions, just like rewards, can foster self-interest. Concerns about the consequences to a child's behaviour become limited to only what will happen to them.

Teachers are creatures of habit. We love our routines and rituals and there is much that is good in this that can be powerful for both adults and children alike in schools. There are touchstones that have been present for what seems like an eternity in our profession – teachers write reports at the end of a year; teachers meet parents at Parents' Evenings in slots of 10 minutes; teachers mark books; the list goes on. Try taking some of those away and we can develop an uncomfortable feeling that something is missing. Some schools have successfully done away with or changed radically some or all of the examples mentioned above, deeming them to be ineffective in supporting children's learning and helpfully reducing teachers' workloads. Good on those schools, but I'll bet there was some nervous hesitation before they took the plunge. How many schools have done the same with some of the sanctions and punishments (I'll stick to the word 'sanction' from now on in this chapter. Remember Bill Rogers from the Introduction – use of 'punishment' is absurd as we're not talking about a prison here) they use that don't actually achieve what they set out do, namely deter children from behaving poorly in the first place or prevent poor behaviour from reoccurring when it does happen? Very few, and there's one major reason why. We feel a visceral urge to do something, anything, swiftly when an incident of poor behaviour occurs. Of course, this is in large part driven by our need to immediately improve the behaviour to prevent disruption to learning both for the child and their classmates and this is entirely right and appropriate. But, because we are creatures of habit, we often reach for sanctions without ever really considering their effectiveness. We have swallowed whole the logic that says because a child did something unpleasant, something unpleasant must be done to them in return. The unpleasantness, so the logic continues, will teach the child a lesson and things will get better. If this were true, behaviour problems would rarely persist and our worst behaved children would respond swiftly to the harshest sanctions. Anyone who has ever worked in schools for children with emotional and behavioural difficulties knows that's not true. The children in those schools have been up the sanctions escalator so many times they've lost count. The rationale here is firmly grounded in the behaviourism that we met in Chapter 5 in the context of rewards. Behaviourism, put simply, contends that behaviours are more likely to recur when we respond by reinforcing the behaviour, or are less likely to recur if we respond to the behaviour by punishing (behaviourism's word, not mine). We can positively reinforce a behaviour by rewarding with something nice or we can reinforce negatively by taking away something unpleasant. Behaviourism says the same about punishment – we can positively punish (this is not an oxymoron, despite it sounding obviously so) by, say, writing a child's name on the board (this is regarded as positive in the sense that something is added) or we can punish negatively by taking something away, like some of their free time in the form of a detention. We feel that if we don't do this then we have somehow let the child get away with it, which offends our sense of justice. You will have already worked out, now that you have got this far into the book, that I believe this to be naïvely simplistic and largely ineffective. Any behaviour policy that relies on behaviourist principles for most or all of its heavy lifting is a plant with very shallow roots indeed. It will be reactionary in nature, and always, therefore, chasing its tail, and ineffective in improving behaviour. It will, however, generate loads of work for teachers in the form of detentions and the like but it is an illusion of action – there's a lot happening, but not much, if anything, is improving; it may even be getting worse. But at least the senior leaders can meet their own needs by saying that they are doing something. As Joe Bower said, 'Are we doing this because it's best for kids? Or because it's convenient for us?'

REFLECTION POINTS

Before we go any further I want you to think about two things:

- What are the sanctions that you habitually use in your day-to-day work?
- Are you doling out those sanctions to the same few children repeatedly? If so, are they actually effective?

What I'm going to attempt in this chapter is to get you to think long and hard about your use of sanctions. I want to get you to focus on trying to improve the behaviour of the children in front of you and to think beyond the urge simply to sanction and move on. (Do not make the mistake of extending my argument that the way we currently use sanctions is ineffective to meaning that I advocate that we do nothing in response to poor behaviour. I don't. I am simply focusing on improving the behaviour.)

Breaking the habit

I mentioned in the introduction how, in the school where I was first a Headteacher, we improved behaviour swiftly, from Ofsted's (and ours) judgement of Requires Improvement to Outstanding in 15 months. This was partly achieved by ceasing to use one major sanction that was ineffective, but on which the school leant very heavily. In the year before I arrived there were 320 sessions of fixed-term exclusion in a school with 120 children in it. This is an eye-wateringly large number and, despite one governor's view that this meant that our behaviour system was working, it was not improving behaviour at all. In fact, quite the opposite. Despite this I did not stop its use immediately, principally because my leadership was weak and I was less confident than I am now in improving behaviour so I continued to respond to big incidents of poor behaviour with exclusion because I was fresh out of ideas. A large part of this was fed by the need to make staff feel supported by a tough response. I was not supporting staff at all in fact, apart from the respite, which is not what responses to poor behaviour should be about. Respite is what weekends are for, and having Saturday and Sunday off school every week doesn't improve the behaviour of children, so it is no surprise that a day or two off in the week doesn't improve behaviour either. The situation was unchanged on the child's return or, in many cases, the relationship between the child and the school had deteriorated because of the rejection caused by the exclusion. When I composed myself I simply stopped using exclusion as a response to poor behaviour. This does not mean that we did nothing in response to poor behaviour. Far from it. It forced us, and this was the point, to consider how best to work with the child to improve their behaviour. It forced us to examine Ross Greene's wise words – children do well if they can, and if they are not doing well they are lacking in skills that their environment demands of them. Simply expecting a child to improve by preventing them from attending school for a time is crossing your fingers and hoping for the best and places all the responsibility on the child. Further, the school and the adults in it need do nothing different, and that is its fundamental weakness. 'Ah yes, but we have reintegration meetings on the child's return so we can plan what to do differently,' I hear you say. Great. Well, just do that anyway and dispense with the idea that the time away from school shocks the child into sorting their life out. In addition, the child misses out on a period of learning time that is lost forever – the worksheets sent home for them to do while they are off are no substitute, assuming, that is, that they are actually completed. I am reminded of Troy, a child who joined our school in Year 7 from a mainstream secondary because they couldn't manage his behaviour. Within three weeks of starting in Year 7 (THREE WEEKS!) Troy was being illegally excluded every day; sent home at 12 o'clock irrespective of how great his behaviour was. I visited him in February and remember with chilling clarity how the SENCo told me, without a hint of irony or responsibility, that they were concerned that Troy was falling behind his peers academically.

Deterrence

One of the common arguments for the continued use of sanctions is that they set an example and deter others from behaving poorly in the future. I have never been persuaded by this argument for a number of reasons. In order to set an example to others the sanction imposed on one child would have to be made public and I sincerely hope schools don't parade sanctions in this way, as shaming is an unnecessary escalation and always counter-productive. For sure, there will be times when some children witness another child receive a sanction (a very small proportion of the whole school remember), but they are unlikely to see the follow through right to its conclusion or all of what happened leading up to it, especially in the more serious cases. You may buy yourself some short-term compliance for things at the minor end of the spectrum such as enforcing uniform standards. For the more serious things that happen in schools such as fights, children swearing at teachers and the like, the severity of whatever sanctions we can impose doesn't actually amount to very much in terms of inconvenience to them. Besides, in the more heated situations children are rarely composed and thinking rationally; they aren't coolly weighing up the pros and cons of their decisions; they aren't making reasoned judgements about the potential consequences of what they are about to do.

Recall from Chapter 2 my feelings about being made to sing or dance. There is virtually no sanction that a school could threaten me with that would incentivise me to do that or deter me from avoiding it. At best, I would do the bare minimum to avoid whatever I was threatened with. Some of the sanctions, such as isolation, would actively help me avoid having to sing or dance, so they immediately lose any deterrent effect and, perversely, offer me a swift way out of what I would consider to be an intolerable situation.

Have you ever broken the speed limit whilst driving? I don't like to make analogies between the behaviour of children in schools and the criminal justice system, but when talking about deterrents speeding does provide some rich comparisons that are worth exploring. Why did you do it? You must know the law, so why did you make the premeditated choice to be naughty? Perhaps you consider yourself to be a brilliant driver (research shows that people often view their own standards as superior[1]) and that you know better than the law? Perhaps you saw it as a victimless crime? Are students breaching certain behaviour rules because, although fully aware they are doing it, they view their infringement as harmless or victimless and therefore without consequence? Uniform infringements or using their mobile phone in lessons may be examples of this.

We all know why speed limits are imposed and that the risk of accidents happening is increased when we speed, yet we still do it. Society ideally wants all drivers to stick to the speed limit or below because it is the right thing to do. We want drivers to be motivated to remain within the law without coercion, and there are two main reasons (one intrinsic and one extrinsic) why someone would do this: (i) they respect other road users, pedestrians and their own passengers enough and value their safety to remain within the law because they recognise that the speed limit is there for that reason; or (ii) despite their view that the speed limit is too low or that their view of their own driving skill means that they were convinced they would remain safe beyond the speed limit they remain within the law because they respect the fact that the law exists and that is enough for them not to break it. In my experience this describes the vast majority of children the vast majority of the time. They respect the rules of the school for what they are – they do the right thing because they want to do the right thing and they are able to do the right thing (revisit Chapter 2 on Bower and Greene and their thoughts on skills gaps). For many there will be rules that they disagree with but they are able to self-regulate and accept the right of the school to set such rules. They stop at the red light even though there isn't another car for miles around. Recalling Chapter 5 on motivation, some are extrinsically motivated because they see themselves as rule-followers and it is the following of the rule, not the fear of what may happen if they break it, that they value, or they actually see real value in the rule itself (such as no running in the corridors or removing their jewellery for PE).

In reality there are some drivers for whom this is true. For the rest the police must enforce the law. They operate various measures to influence the behaviour of drivers. We extrinsically motivate them to remain within the law by erecting speed cameras in accident blackspots that catch speeding drivers resulting in a fine and some penalty points on their licence. And how do these cameras influence the behaviour of drivers exactly? Drivers tend to slow down in the vicinity of the camera. And what do they do immediately afterwards? That's right, they tend to speed up again. This is the equivalent of the morning uniform check on the school gate – just before the child rounds the corner into school the skirt and tie are returned to regulation length (eight stripes – no more, no less) and the shirt tucked in. Once out of sight of the Headteacher the skirt is hitched up, the tie shortened and the shirt untucked once more. Repeat *ad nauseum* throughout the day.

This enforcement method is limited so police officers use more agile methods such as speed guns and traffic cars equipped with detection equipment which can be deployed anywhere. Certain types of vehicles have speed limiters on them (heavy goods vehicles and school minibuses, for example) as surefire methods of prevention. You couldn't speed even if you wanted to. If your school has branded rucksacks, trousers and skirts then this is a road down which you have gone. Specifying exactly what legwear is to be worn seeks to remove the chance that children could fall foul of your rules. The same is true when mobile phones must be handed in. Both underestimate the ingenuity of children who may hand in one phone, but keep another in their bag.

In spite of all this, speeding remains a fact of life. Why? Drivers are carrying out a risk assessment that sometimes falls down on the side of breaking the law. Benefits might be that they will get there quicker or that they like driving fast. Risks might be the weather, the safety of other road users, the chance of getting caught and the subsequent fine and points. The analysis changes when they approach a speed camera or see a police car so their behaviour changes for as long as the risks outweigh the benefits, and their behaviour changes once more when the chance of being caught diminishes below an acceptable level. Some children do the same when assessing the chances of being seen or caught doing something that they know they shouldn't, such as using their phone in a lesson. It is not solely the existence of the sanction that deters, it is a combination of the sanction set against the likelihood of being caught. The harshest punishment imaginable will not deter if you are pretty certain that you will get away with whatever it is you know that you should not be doing.

This is where the element of certainty comes in. Teachers with presence, one of the most-prized of teacher superpowers, radiate a sense of vigilance – not hyper-vigilance, though, which makes children and other adults edgy as the most minor of infractions, which could be safely ignored, become major events. The children are sure that this teacher sees everything and will not let anything go that they, and everyone around them, know is unacceptable. These teachers are not the harshest, scariest types out there. They are the ones whose expectations never slip, which is why they always seem to be serenely in control. They nip almost everything in the bud and rarely need to resort to more overt tactics to sort behaviour problems.

Puffing penguins

I remember when I first started teaching one of my pet hates was doing break duty. I have since grown to love break and lunch duties, especially as a senior leader, but as an NQT I regarded them as an inconvenience that got in the way of setting up my lab for my next lesson. One reason I hated them was the never-ending battle, or so it felt, with the small number of determined, tenacious and resourceful smokers amongst our student population. They had their tactics honed through years of experience, younger ones learning from veterans by being taken, almost literally as you will see in a moment, under their wing. In common with many secondary schools built in the 1960s, our school contained much dead ground between the different departmental blocks – perfect turf for an illicit fag before cross-country. Their brazen disregard for the rules, their own health and the example they were setting to others – there is little that is more disconcerting than seeing a child smoking – irritated me, but our seemingly casual acceptance as a school that they were doing it irritated me far more.

The rule in school was clear – smoking was banned, as was possession of the materials required to do it. Being caught smoking theoretically led to one of two things – a one-day exclusion or a 'stop smoking' course. From my lowly position as an NQT I never got to see up close and personal how often this happened, but I could judge the effectiveness of these sanctions, and of addiction, because the same children were there, day after day. Part of their brazenness was because their risk assessment on the likelihood of being caught came out on the low side. You would think that spotting a child smoking in a school would be an easy task, but they were well organised. Imagine a huddle of penguins all taking it in turns to spend time on the outside taking the brunt of the Antarctic wind. Inside that huddle were a number of children smoking away, individually almost invisible to the outside world and well protected, until it was their turn to shield their mates from the elements. The chance of being seen was low, but you had to catch someone at it and you couldn't resort to a corporate punishment as there were some children there who were non-smokers and were there for the company. I had no hold on the school policy, but I could do something about my area of responsibility. I simply resorted to planting myself on duty right in the middle of their favoured smokers' corner. I used to go to the Millennium Garden and stand on top of the concrete bench right in the middle, which was their preferred spot. I had a view down one entire side of the school, so they had to go elsewhere. I knew that I couldn't control that – it needed a concerted effort from all of us on duty to take the same approach to policing known problem areas – but it was effective in removing it as a problem from my area. I was the teacher version of the speed camera in the earlier analogy. I changed their behaviour for as long as they were within my sphere of influence. Once beyond my view, just as with the speed camera, their risk assessment changed and so did their behaviour. The clear rules and unambiguous sanctions were not a deterrent. Being caught was a risk worth taking unless we as a staff could get our break duty coverage right; the combination of the craving brought on by addiction, the pull of the social occasion and the thrill of flagrantly flouting school rules, with the kudos that bought with some peers, all outweighed the inconvenience, or reward, depending on your point of view, of a one-day exclusion (which was far less hassle than a smoking cessation course which few, if any, opted for).

Productive and restorative sanctions

I am not arguing for you to stop using sanctions in response to poor behaviour. I am arguing that what you choose to do in response to poor behaviour if you think a sanction is necessary needs to be productive. If it isn't we are meeting our own short-term needs, because we feel the need to say we did something, ideally something that sounds tough. Productive also does not mean relying on the lost free time and the inconvenience doing the persuading for the child to change their ways. It won't, for anything other than the most minor of issues.

So what kind of sanctions do we commonly resort to using? It depends on the age of the children, as primary schools are relatively light on sanctions when compared to secondaries, but they largely amount to removing free time, property or access to something from a child. We remove time from children in the form of detention, and this has many varieties: break time, lunchtime, after school, Headteachers' and Saturday detention, for example. This hierarchy of detentions gives the appearance of an increase in severity, but in essence it is largely window-dressing. The child is still simply being inconvenienced, but for longer – Headteacher and Saturday detentions tend to be for longer periods of time and in some cases the inconvenience spreads to the parents as they may have to collect the child and or bring them in on the Saturday. Detentions are blunt; their inconvenience is supposed to be its deterrent. I believe we would get far more out of detentions if we made them much shorter and used them to do some intensive restorative work with the child. If they have work to catch up on, they can then finish it, or it's agreed that they do it that night if possible, and you're done. Read on to Chapter 7 for more on what restorative conversations look like, particularly playground or corridor restorations. This is unpopular with many teachers as we know it inevitably adds to our own workload. But, done properly, incidents reduce over time anyway, with the total teacher time devoted to detentions reducing. Unfortunately the unpalatable truth is this – if we don't take the lead we are relying on hope. We don't own the behaviour of the child, but we can certainly do a lot to help them make it better.

REFLECTION POINTS

- Reflect on the detention system in use in your school.

- Make a rough estimate of the time consumed by this system each week.

- How could that time be used more effectively when explicitly directed at improving behaviour?

Sending children out of the classroom for a time, or to isolation, or the Reflection Room (mirrorless, I'll bet) as I've heard it called, are just as blunt. Far better to use a short period of time outside of the classroom to talk to a child away from an audience. If there is a need for anything more than a restatement of expectations to a child then removing the audience is a good idea – the child can save face (don't underestimate how powerful this can be; losing face never de-escalates a situation). Besides, having a child outside the classroom on their own poses two risks: firstly, they simply get bored and walk off; and secondly, they play the clown through the window to their classmates or to other classes, neither of which helps you, them or the rest of the class. Engage, make your point firmly and move on.

Confiscation is a common response to misuse of property such as a mobile phone or the presence of prohibited items such as fidget spinners or trading cards. This can also be a very effective deterrent in the short term as loss aversion tends to buy temporary compliance. The thought of losing their mobile phone for a period of time can be a powerful, temporary corrective for a child but the urge to use it remains. I was Headteacher of a secondary special school that was small enough for us to keep all of the children's mobile phones during the day and this worked really well. It was obvious to us when one student had not handed theirs in and we could enforce our rules. Much harder in a secondary school with well over a thousand children, each with a phone. The best schools I know have very clear expectations and enforce them rigorously. They don't expect phones to be visible during the school day without the express permission of the teacher. If they are seen when they shouldn't be out they are confiscated for a short period of time (confiscation for weeks on end is unnecessary, builds resentment and is likely to fall foul of the lightest of legal challenges). Of course, a child can refuse to hand over property that you wish to confiscate, in which case consideration can be given as to whether the child is allowed the phone, or whatever it is, in school for a longer period or at all. Again, loss aversion can be effective here and is likely to lead to short-term compliance. Far better to work on the assumption that the children can be responsible and mature, whilst being clear about what will happen if they fall below that, than to resort to an outright ban on the basis that the children can't or won't do the right thing.

The last type of sanction we tend to use involves restricting access or removal of a privilege. Remember the example from Chapter 5 where children had to earn the right to attend their prom? This is another blunt response, and not one that is aimed at the problem. It is from the behaviourist school of thought once more – removal of something nice will result in improved behaviour. I doubt it very much, but it is used commonly. 'You can't represent the school at football if you can't behave in class!' Why? A child might be a tremendous ambassador for the school on the football field and it could be a great way of building up their emotional investment in their school. Removing that on the basis that it will extrinsically motivate them to behave well in some other area of school life is nonsensical. Far better to address the problem where it resides than to resort to a hit-and-hope response. You are highly unlikely to improve behaviour in this way. It is classic 'I win, you lose' territory. You will feel better because you have gone 1–0 up, but you can be fairly confident that you will increase resentment, another unnecessary escalation.

REFLECTION POINTS

- Do you remove privileges as part of your behaviour policy?
- What are you trying to achieve by doing this?
- Could these sanctions be in areas of school life where children are at their most successful?

Extra work

Be careful that you don't give the impression that school work is a form of punishment. Catching up on work that has been missed because of poor behaviour is a smart use of time. I wouldn't sell this as a sanction though. Completing the work, because it was a basic expectation that the work would be done anyway, is a consequence of lost learning time, not a sanction imposed afterwards. Piling on extra work to increase the unpleasantness only adds to the message that work is a chore and fosters resentment. An evolution of this tactic is to make a child do extra work as a sanction when the rest of the class are enjoying Golden Time or similar. Watching peers having a good time whilst the child is sat alone working is supposed to be a bitter medicine that induces the child to behave better in the future. Refer back to Chapter 2 – we don't remove access to subjects we think the child won't like. I've heard 'If you don't behave you can't go swimming this afternoon!' and have had to explain to unhappy teachers that they can't remove access to swimming as a sanction, but strangely I am yet to hear 'If you don't behave you won't get homework tonight!' The curriculum is an entitlement and is not something to be traded or used as a negotiating tool or bargaining chip.

Shaming

Every time we write a child's name on the board in response to poor behaviour we run the risk of escalating a situation by shaming them. Why else are we doing it? We are trying to embarrass the child into behaving, and that never ends well. The old me would say that I am placing a reminder to the child that their behaviour is falling below an acceptable level, but I could just tell them that (see Chapter 11 for how I recklessly misused our school's behaviour system when I first started teaching). We do the same when we use traffic light systems. The majority of the children remain on the green light because their behaviour is good, and then there will be the same few flitting between green and amber with the occasional forays in to the red. Traffic light systems are endemic in classrooms, but entirely unnecessary. If you have one stick it in the bin now. The children who habitually reside on the green light are not there because the traffic light is helping them remain there. They will behave well, traffic light system or not. Yours may have words next to it, but I hope it is nothing like the worst example I've ever seen. With a title DISCIPLINED DELIGHT! each traffic light had a name – green was labelled COOPERATIVE, amber BREAKS RULES and red APPALLING. What a welcoming classroom to be in.

Shaming generates strong feelings and tends to provoke a combination of behaviours, none of which is helpful or productive (Elison et al., 2006).[2] It breaks our 'do not escalate' mantra and should be avoided at all costs. You may see:

- **Withdrawal** – this could be introversion or physical withdrawal by, for example, leaving your lesson.
- **Denial (also called avoidance)** – this could be the classic 'I DON'T CARE!' or by laughing. In reality the child is seeking to minimise or deny the negative experience.
- **Attacking themselves** – the child turns their negative feelings inwards, which can magnify them, and they may feel low self-worth, call themselves 'stupid' or feel contempt for themselves.
- **Attacking others** – the child turns their negative feelings outwards and, as with denial, this can be an attempt to minimise the feeling of shame by blaming someone else – you or another child, for example.

You can see that shaming is entirely counter-productive. We are seeking to humanely correct behaviour, not shame a child into changing.

We run the risk of shaming with overt responses such as lining up in assembly children who are improperly dressed. It is done to set an example to others – the children who would be petrified of lining up at the front of assembly are probably immaculately dressed anyway, they're rule followers – but it shames, and I have seen children ape a Headteacher behind his back whilst they stand there (classic shaming denial).

Teacher empathy

There is some interesting recent research from Okonofua et al. (2016)[3] from Stanford University showing that when teachers approach problems of poor behaviour with strategies and responses that encourage mutual understanding and respect, they can reduce incidents of poor behaviour and prevent the escalation of conflict that often leads to exclusion. In essence, the researchers examined punitive approaches to solving behavioural problems against empathetic approaches, noticing that an empathetic approach discouraged teachers from applying labels to the children such as 'troublemaker' (remember Chapter 2 on psychology and how we need to avoid labelling). This makes obvious sense to me, given that a punitive or behaviourist approach will tend to take a deficit view – the child is the problem – whereas empathy fosters an urge to support the child to behave better and to identify what it will take to help them do this. This finding should be set against the work of Hemphill et al. (2017),[4] who demonstrated that suspension, one of the most punitive responses we can use, increased the likelihood of problem behaviour in children, including violent and anti-social behaviour, disconcertingly called deviance amplification, feeding the depressingly named school-to-prison pipeline.

What's in it for me?

In Chapter 5 we looked at one of the major weaknesses of rewards, namely that they can foster self-interest. The task or work at hand is done, or the child behaves, only in order to receive the reward. Rewards may buy some short-term compliance, or the child may half-heartedly do the minimum to secure the Vivo points or some such. Sanctions are no different. They can focus the mind of the child on doing the bare minimum that it will take to keep the teacher off their back. Work is a chore to get out of the way as quickly as possible in order to keep their free time. Sanctions are short-term tactics, but you will never get buy-in or emotional investment from a child. You cannot punish a child into caring about you, their peers or a particular subject. When we talk about the consequences of behaving in a certain way this becomes narrowed to the consequences to that particular child. This is why blunt use of sanctions will only ever be limited, both in terms of time and endurance, in their effort to improve behaviour unless we use them restoratively. The sheer amount of dead time that our limited repertoire of sanctions burns each week could be used far more effectively if we used them as opportunities to help children understand the effects of their behaviour on themselves and everyone else involved. If we don't, sanctions just become part and parcel of school life for some children as they ricochet from one detention to another, with members of staff shaking their heads disconsolately that those children never learn.

TAKING IT FURTHER – QUESTIONS AND ACTIVITIES FOR YOU AND YOUR COLLEAGUES

- Make three lists:
  - All the sanctions you currently use in your school.
  - The staff time absorbed every week by each one.
  - The children who are regularly receiving these sanctions.

- Ask yourselves, are we content that (a) this is a productive use of staff time; (b) these sanctions are leading to improvements in the behaviour of the children who are ever-present on the detention list?

- If we have concerns about the effectiveness of our current system to encourage behaviour improvements, what can we do instead?

- Should we be reducing the dead time consumed by detentions and devote the time to restorative work instead?

- What kind of system would we need to set up in order for this be successful?

- Are there any aspects of our behaviour policy, or of our own personal classroom practice, that lean on shaming or embarrassing children into compliance?
    - Do we write names on the board as a form of warning?
    - Do we use a public traffic light system or similar?
    - What can we do instead?

- Do we use school work to increase the unpleasantness of sanctions?

References

1   Roy, M.M. and Liersch, M.J. (2014) 'I am a better driver than you think: examining self-enhancement for driving ability', *Journal of Applied Social Psychology*, 43 (8): 1648–59.

2   Elison, J., Lennon, R. and Pulos, S. (2006) 'Investigating the Compass of Shame: the development of the Compass of Shame scale', *Social Behavior and Personality*, 34 (3): 221–38.

3   Okonofua, J., Paunesku, D. and Walton, G. (2016) 'Brief intervention to encourage empathic discipline cuts suspension rates in half among adolescents', *Proceedings of the National Academic of Sciences of the United States of America*, 113 (19): 5221–6.

4   Hemphill, S., Broderick, D. and Heerde, J. (2017) 'Positive associations between school suspension and student problem behaviour: a summary of recent Australian findings', *Trends and Issues in Crime and Criminal Justice*, 531: 1–13.

7

RESTORATIVE APPROACHES TO PREVENTING AND RESOLVING CONFLICT

'I'm sorry' is a statement.

'I won't do it again' is a promise.

'How do I make it up to you?' is a responsibility.

Mark Finnis, Restorative Practices trainer

THE HEADLINES

- Restorative practices aim to:
  - provide a safe and secure space for children who have been harmed to communicate the impact of that on them;
  - improve behaviour of those causing harm by allowing children to understand the impact of their behaviour on others;
  - seek solutions by working with children rather than imposing solutions upon them;
  - help children take responsibility for their behaviour and be accountable for their actions.
- Restorative practices are not soft alternatives to punishment.
- They are hard to do well and they can need an investment in time (like all effective behaviour strategies).
- There are six principles to restorative practices:
  - restoration;
  - voluntarism;
  - neutrality;
  - safety;
  - accessibility;
  - respect.
- Restorative work is based on gathering information, establishing impact on the people involved and facilitating those involved to seek solutions.

- Restorative practices allow for ambiguity where blame is hard to establish.

- There are a range of strategies you can employ:
    - affective statements;
    - affective questions;
    - impromptu restoration (so-called playground or corridor restorations);
    - group or circle time;
    - formal restorative conferences.

Incidents between human beings happen in schools all the time. Children fall out with each other, sometimes over what we perceive to be petty issues, sometimes over things that are more serious; unfortunately, children sometimes bully other children; sometimes children and adults come into conflict. The schools that I know where behaviour is best are not the ones who claim that this sort of thing never happens (I'm concerned that those schools are worried that to admit that it happens is a sign of weakness), it is the ones that have a strong culture of mutual respect and a collective pride in their school that minimises such incidents, and well-trained staff with effective policies and procedures to deal with these issues when they do arise. I am extremely wary of any school that claims, for example, that they have no bullying, and I know a few who do make this claim.

These effective schools are also the ones who are not relying on outward displays of toughness after incidents have happened, relying on the thin hope that this will deter others from doing the same. They are the schools that are building cultures from the ground up based on respect for fellow humans, and for the environment of the school itself, ideally in order to prevent conflict arising in the first place and resolving conflict when it does unfortunately happen. And when it does happen, their aim is to deal with relationship-damaging situations between people such that those issues don't persist and instances reduce over time. This is the essence of restorative practices in schools.

Restorative practices create sufficient time and a safe space to enable those who have been harmed to communicate the impact of that harm to those responsible. Further, it aims for those responsible to appreciate, understand and acknowledge the impact of their actions on others and to take steps to repair the situation and relationship (think feedback as information as opposed to reward and punishment, as per the quote by Jerome Bruner at the start of Chapter 5). This appreciation, understanding and acknowledgement is clearly intended to lead to changes in behaviour so that disagreements and conflicts are settled and resolved amicably and maturely in the future or, ideally, they don't recur at all. These practices promote and support children doing the right thing because it is the right thing to do, rather than only doing the right thing in order to avoid a punishment.

The use of restorative practices in schools has, in my view at the current time, a bit of an image problem. Some teachers I speak to regard it as soft and progressive (in the pejorative sense) and a dressed-up version of a cosy chat for a child that needs to be punished. They instinctively reject it as a strategy in the same way that I immediately reject suggestions to bring back corporal punishment because, so I hear, it would instil discipline in today's children and, besides, they got a beating at school and it didn't do them any harm. I suspect that this recoil is at least partly grounded in our cultural history of the use of punishment. For example, as a country we imprison more children than many of our European cousins[1] (interestingly England and Wales have the lowest age of criminal responsibility of any country in Europe, at 10 years old[2]), and I see a visceral reaction from people in society, the same being true of teachers in schools, if they feel that someone has not been made to suffer as a result of their wrongdoing. As I have said a couple of times in this book already, it is an example of how in certain situations we are meeting our own needs as opposed to asking how best can this situation be resolved so that it doesn't happen again. The punishment/deterrence school of thought takes a rather dim view of the children in our schools, insofar as it suggests that without the presence of deterrents or severe consequences children in schools will simply run amok, safe in the knowledge that they can get away with things as long as they are prepared to have a cosy chat with the Headteacher afterwards. This makes me sad and doesn't remind me of the overwhelming majority of children I've ever met. Surely we want children to do the right thing because it's the right thing to do? Children do well if they can, as Ross Greene says, and restorative practices aim to prevent the reoccurrence of conflict and harm by changing the behaviour of children in order to do better in situations where they haven't in the past.

The other main criticism or concern I hear about the use of restorative practices is that it forces victims to share time and space with someone who has harmed them. This is felt even more strongly if a restorative meeting is between a member of staff and a child, as the member of staff may feel that they and the child are being treated as equals and regard this as demeaning. You will see below that one of the key principles of restorative practices is that the process is entirely voluntary. People cannot be coerced into taking part, so it can be a challenge to convince people that it will be effective (success cannot be guaranteed, like all responses and interventions) and to put their trust in you if they are initially sceptical. Ultimately, it is the outcomes from the restorative process that will change people's minds and to get that far they have to be prepared to go through the process. People don't tend to feel this way about punitive reactions to conflict, because they are generally satisfied that someone has been punished, even if behaviour doesn't subsequently change and the punishment was a knee-jerk response to the call that 'something must be done!'

There is persuasive evidence out there, though, such as the DfE's *The Use and Effectiveness of Anti-Bullying Strategies in Schools* report,[3] which notes that 97% of the schools involved in the report found restorative approaches to be effective in reducing bullying.

Lastly, the image problem of restorative work persists because, like all strategies that lead to long-lasting behaviour change, it takes time and is not easy to do well, so people give up. Detentions, exclusions and other punitive responses are simple and easy to execute, which is why people like me reach for them in times of stress when we're facing calls to 'do something, and fast, to sort this kid out!' You will see, though, that restorative approaches are far more than formal, sit-down meetings. Ultimately restorative approaches are a philosophy and a way of working and communicating, not a tool to pull out of your bag when you're at the end of your tether. You will see in this chapter that the approaches range from the everyday language you use in the classroom in the form of informal affective statements up to full-blown formal restorative conferences.

REFLECTION POINTS

- What is your school's response to conflict and bullying? How restorative do you think it is?

- Does it aim to change behaviour by allowing children to understand the impact of their behaviour on others?

Principles of restorative practice

There are a set of underlying principles upon which effective restorative work is based.

1. **Restoration** – The primary objective of restorative practice is quite clearly to address and repair harm.
2. **Voluntarism** – People cannot be forced to participate in restorative approaches. This does mean it is important that people know what they are letting themselves in for, what they are committing to and what their responsibilities are. The first formal restorative process that I was involved in ended prematurely because the child (Stephen from the Introduction who punched me in the head – see later in this chapter for further details) withdrew part way through.

3. **Neutrality** – Restorative approaches need to be fair and unbiased towards participants. If they are considered to be another forum in which to hector a child, a *fait accompli*, or a thinly veiled form of court, then this risks the process breaking down or, at the very least, being less effective.

4. **Safety** – If a child has been harmed by another then it cannot be easy for them to sit down and talk through the emotions, the hurt and the after-effects in their presence unless they can be confident that it is safe to do so. This will involve some preparation on your part as you may need to give careful consideration to the details, such as the location; for instance, the Headteacher's office can be considered to be a very intimidating place for some children.

5. **Accessibility** – Restorative work is non-discriminatory and must be available to all those affected by conflict and harm. For example, you will read later on in Chapter 10 about the overlap between speech, language and communication difficulties and behavioural difficulties in children. We must be careful to ensure our language is accessible to the children we do restorative work with and appreciate that they may struggle to communicate their own feelings, or they may struggle to recall the chronology of events successfully. They may, too, find it difficult to truly understand the effects of their own behaviour on another person – this is a strong argument for the use of restorative practices, not a reason to dismiss them as a resolution strategy – and require support with that.

6. **Respect** – Restorative practices must be respectful to the dignity of all participants and those affected by the harm caused. It is not a forum to shame the person causing harm as, again, this is likely to reduce the effectiveness of the process.

REFLECTION POINT

- How does your current practice when dealing with conflict and bullying measure up against the six principles? Is there anything you need to do differently?

Stephen

My first experience of the use of formal restorative practice to resolve a conflict ended in failure. It came about after I was punched in the head by Stephen. I'd worked at our school for children with behavioural difficulties for a couple of months and had built some really good relationships with most of the children in that time. I taught Stephen both GCSE maths and science and it is fair to say that I was not his favourite teacher. One afternoon I was entering the main building, laptop in one hand, lever arch file in the other, and Stephen ran from one end of the car park to the other, shouting 'I'm gonna smash your fucking head in!' I was a serving Special Constable at this point, so you would think I was well placed to handle this, especially as he'd told me exactly what he was going to do, but I just stood stock still as I was convinced he wouldn't hit me, and then remained rooted to the spot as he punched me in the head.

The upshot was that the Headteacher called the police, Stephen was arrested on suspicion of common assault and taken away. After school I was asked by the Headteacher what I wanted to happen next and I said, genuinely, that I wanted him in the next day so that we could get started on fixing this relationship problem. The police were doing their thing – they cautioned him, which was a proportionate and sensible response – and I didn't see any sense in waiting to resolve the problem; indeed, I felt that waiting would only make things worse. You may regard this as ill-advised or naïve; remember, though, that he was at a school for children with extreme behavioural difficulties and had been permanently excluded from two other schools for violence. He had been to the top of the punishment escalator many times with little or no sign of improvement. I wasn't excusing his behaviour; I just wanted it to improve and I knew that wouldn't be achieved by a punishment from the school. He received a fixed-term exclusion (that is to say, he was suspended and not allowed to be in school) for 45 days instead – the maximum amount of time a child can be excluded for in any one academic year, either in one period or cumulatively if they are excluded a number of times. I am sure that was one of the reasons why the restorative work carried out later was less effective; far too much time had passed between the incident and the meeting – nine school weeks, plus a half-term – for it to mean anything.

A formal restorative meeting was organised as part of Stephen's reintegration and it was hosted by a superb colleague from the local authority, a former Metropolitan Police officer. Stephen's parents were present at the meeting too, which I considered a good idea as he could easily have felt outnumbered. Everyone involved had a chance to speak uninterrupted, and I would have had a chance to explain how I'd been affected by the incident, with a focus then on what needed to happen so that we could move on. Stephen walked out of the room before we really got going because he found the formal nature of it too much to cope with, too much time had passed since the incident and we hadn't done enough preparation for him to understand what was going to happen and why.

Stephen and I got there in the end – that incident was the low-point in our relationship. He got his maths and science GCSEs and we got on, although, understandably, I had to make all the running to start with. I knew that I had to make the emotional investment in him and our relationship first and that it wasn't going to be fixed overnight. I had to resort to more informal restorative means (not all restorative strategies have to be formal, sit-down affairs and, indeed, so-called corridor restoration can remove the rigid nature of more formal means) to show him I was not going to give up on him, that I understood his stressors and that I liked him and wanted him to be successful. This was, of course, not easy, because he fully expected me to hold the incident against him forever. In short, I had to work with him and start from where he was, not impose something upon him.

TO – NOT – FOR – WITH – 'no about us without us'

Part of the foundation of restorative approaches is the belief that people are more likely to change their behaviour for the better when those in positions of authority do things *with* them rather than *to* them or *for* them.

The Social Discipline Window (Figure 7.1) helps us to understand how restorative approaches require a balance of high levels of control and limit-setting with high levels of support, encouragement and nurture.

High control and low support creates a punitive, stigmatising and author-itarian environment and amounts to doing things *to* people, and we all know as teachers how uppity we get when Headteachers or the government try to impose things upon us without our involvement. There's a saying in special schools about working with children with learning difficulties that sums this up well – no about us without us.

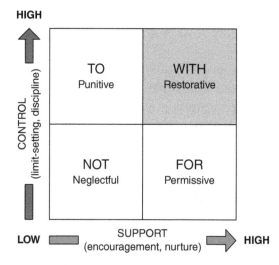

Figure 7.1 The Social Discipline Window (reproduced by permission of the International Institute of Restorative Practices, 'Defining Restorative' www.iirp.edu)

Low control and low support results in a neglectful and irresponsible environment and amounts to the adults *not* doing much at all. This is dangerous because people can feel exposed by the lack of security this engenders and no one, not even the adults, take responsibility for anything.

High support and low control leads to a permissive and paternalistic environment where those in authority are doing things *for* people. It is difficult to get people to take personal responsibility for anything if they are overprotected and have learned that there is little or no expectation of them.

High support and high control creates a restorative environment which prioritises doing things *with* people. This is important, because when support is high the threat that participants can feel drops, but only when the limits are clearly set so they are secure about the level of expectation of their involvement. Remember too that restorative strategies involve holding people to account and the environment must be safe and secure for this to happen.

The restorative practices continuum

If you have heard of restorative approaches to resolving conflict in the past you may automatically think of a formal meeting, but there is much more to it than that. Indeed, when a teacher or, ideally, a school, adopts restorative practices as their default setting they are likely to rarely feel the need to resort to formal restorative conferences.

Restorative practices include any response to harm, wrong-doing or conflict or, more importantly, any ways of communicating and working with children that actively foster mutual respect, concern for others and collaborative problem-solving that prevent conflict or make it less likely.

As such they range from the kind of language that you as the adult regularly use in the form of unplanned affective statements, right up to well-planned conferences, as shown in Figure 7.2.

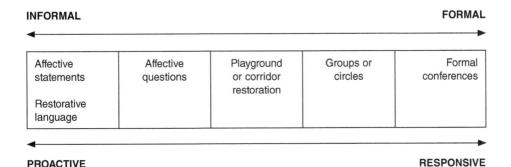

INFORMAL → FORMAL

Affective statements	Affective questions	Playground or corridor restoration	Groups or circles	Formal conferences
Restorative language				

PROACTIVE ← → RESPONSIVE

Figure 7.2 The restorative practices continuum

At one end of the continuum there are affective statements in which one person communicates to another the impact of their behaviour – 'You're taking learning time away from the rest of the class, which is unfair.' No response is expected necessarily, but they are enough to make the impact clear to the child and are more beneficial than a 'Will you be quiet!' You might use these for low-level disruption and they may need to be followed later by an affective question at an appropriate time, perhaps asking, 'How do you think Becky felt when you did that?' Both statements and questions are intended to provoke reflection from the child on how their behaviour has affected others.

Restorative practices trainer Mark Finnis suggests a very helpful template for affective statements:

'When you [behaviour] I feel [impact]. What I need is [what you need them to do].'

This can be short and sweet, such as 'When you talk when I am talking to the class I feel frustrated because you're disrupting the learning of others who are ready. I need you to stop talking and listen.' Affective statements can also buy you some time and make it clear that this will be revisited in a few minutes, such as 'When you [behaviour] I feel [impact]. What I need to do is talk this through with you later/outside for a minute/after the lesson.' You can then have a restorative conversation in a little more depth away from the audience that is the rest of the class.

REFLECTION POINT

- Try to increase your use of affective statements and questions in your responses to low-level disruption and minor issues in the classroom to replace emptier statements and commands.

Playground or corridor restoration is where I have done most overt restorative work. This work is impromptu and in response to relatively minor issues of conflict or disagreement, and these things tend to happen more often at times in schools when supervision is thinner on the ground and children have more free time on their hands, namely at lesson changeover times, before and after school and at break and lunch times, hence the name. This work is swift, aiming to resolve things there and then, and not used for persistent issues. I follow a simple format:

- **Gather information from everyone** – 'What happened? Do you agree with that? Anything to add?'
- **Establish impact** – 'Who has been affected by this? How?'
- **Solution** – 'What do you need to do to fix this? What about you? Both happy? Right. Both see me tomorrow morning and we'll see how you've got on.'

There is a better chance that minor things don't then spill over into lessons or persist if they are nipped in the bud and all involved can move on feeling that a situation has been resolved satisfactorily. As a Headteacher I ensured I was around at lesson changeovers wherever possible and did break, lunch and after-school duty every day I was in school too. This enabled me to resolve many smaller incidents such as fallings-out on the football pitch, basketball court or on the climbing equipment straight away. If I did, though, I always tried to make sure that the receiving teacher knew that something had happened and what we had done to resolve it, in case there were problems. It helped them stay alert for tensions that could flare up or make sense of comments that might be made.

All of these informal and impromtu processes should have a cumulative effect as they become part-and-parcel of the everyday language and slip into 'the way we do things round here'.

REFLECTION POINT

- You won't have to do to many duties before you are needed to step in to resolve a problem between two children. Try the *gather information* → *establish impact* → *find solutions* restorative approach and try to gauge its effectiveness over time.

For persistent problems or for more serious incidents you may need to resort to restorative work for a group (sometimes called *circles*, something that primary schools tend to be very good at in the form of circle time), such as when an issue arises with a number of children through the inappropriate use of social media, or a more formal conference to resolve bullying, for example.

Groups or circles are a good alternative to formal conferences when there is no clear person causing harm to another or others, or you want to avoid a potential win/lose situation. Groups allow everyone the opportunity to speak and to listen in a safe environment, free from interruption. They do need to be managed and sometimes a 'talk piece' is used to signify the one person who is allowed to speak to prevent a free-for-all. Unlike formal conferences they can be set up very quickly, and, although more flexible in nature, they generally follow the structure detailed below.

Formal conferences need to be planned in advance and consideration does need to be given to who needs to attend, where the conference will be held and the needs of the attendees (such as a child or children with learning difficulties) to get the best outcome. When I chaired my first two or three restorative conferences I stuck to a script rigidly to ensure I did it right, but they all felt a bit stilted. Those I did subsequently were more fluid as I gained confidence and was able to respond more flexibly to the information the children were divulging. There are two basic structures to conferences that I have used. One is the same as that for playground restorations: gather information – establish impact – find a solution. Within that three-part structure each of the participants is spoken to before moving on to the next. The other format asks questions of the person(s) who caused harm first, then asks questions of the person(s) who had been harmed, before finally eliciting from those harmed what they would like the outcome of the conference to be. I prefer to gather information from everyone before moving on to the next bit as, in my experience, you inevitably go back to that stage when the second or later participants have their chance to speak.

There is an array of questions you can ask (see below), and note that they tend to be open questions, designed to elicit information as opposed to securing agreement or resulting in yes/no answers. Clearly the language used in the questions, the number of questions to ask and the communication and cognitive abilities of the children taking part are vital considerations in choosing what questions to ask. In my experience, it is also important to provide sufficient processing time to allow children to compose their answers. Don't be tempted to fill silences or to continually rephrase questions either.

Suggested questions for gathering information

- 'What happened?'
- 'Tell us about the situation that brought us here today?'
- 'What happened before that?'
- 'And then what happened?'
- 'What do you think about that now?'
- 'What were you thinking at the time?'
- 'What did you see?'

- 'What did you hear?'
- 'What did you say?'
- 'Who was there?'
- 'What were you thinking about at the time?'
- 'What have you thought about since the incident?'

Suggested questions for establishing impact

- 'How have you been affected by this?'
- 'Who has been affected by this?'
- 'How have they been affected?'
- 'How do you feel about the situation now?'
- 'What has been the hardest thing for you?'

Suggested questions for finding solutions

- 'What needs to happen now?'
- 'What do you need to move on from this?'
- 'What could you do to repair this relationship?'
- 'When will that happen?'
- 'Is that suggestion OK with you?'
- 'Do you agree with that?'
- 'If you can't do that, what can you do?'

Go back to Mark Finnis' wise words at the start of this chapter. Much of what we do in schools in trying to tackle poor behaviour remains rooted in punitive responses by doing things *to* children, rather than working *with* them to help them become more responsible and accountable for their own actions and choices. Restorative work provides a way of involving children who would be passive recipients under punitive systems. In restorative work children take an active part and help decide how to repair situations.

Restorative processes are also good at coping with ambiguity, given that in some situations it can be difficult to ascertain where fault lies. Indeed, as I mentioned in Chapter 2, there are often problems to be solved on both sides of a conflict and the children must feel like you care about helping them to solve their problems as much as you care about solving your own or someone elses.

Lastly, restorative approaches to resolving conflict regard every negative situation as an opportunity for learning and for personal growth and are explicitly designed to strive for that in a way that summary punitive responses can never do.

TAKING IT FURTHER – QUESTIONS AND ACTIVITIES FOR YOU AND YOUR COLLEAGUES

- As a school are we ready to embrace restorative principles?

- If so, what training do we need?

- What is our current approach to dealing with bullying?

- Is our approach to dealing with minor issues consistent with restorative principles?

- Do our lunch time supervisors need training in order to deal with minor issues in a restorative way?

- What training and support do we provide for our peer mediators?

References

1 Council of Europe Annual Penal Statistics, *SPACE I – Prison Populations Survey 2015*, p. 58. http://wp.unil.ch/space/files/2017/04/SPACE_I_2015_FinalReport_161215_REV170425.pdf (accessed 11 December 2017).

2 *Do England and Wales Imprison More Children than Any other Countries in Europe?* Full Fact website. https://fullfact.org/news/do-england-and-wales-imprison-more-children-any-other-countries-europe/ (accessed 11 December 2017).

3 Thompson, F. and Smith, Peter K. (2011) *The Use and Effectiveness of Anti-Bullying Strategies in Schools*. DFE-RR098. London: Department for Education. p. 94. Available at www.gov.uk/government/uploads/system/uploads/attachment_data/file/182421/DFE-RR098.pdf (accessed 11 December 2017).

8

WORKING IN PARTNERSHIP WITH PARENTS TO IMPROVE BEHAVIOUR

Cooperation is the thorough conviction that nobody can get there unless everybody gets there.

Virginia Burden

THE HEADLINES

- Working together with parents to improve behaviour is most effective when parents are respected and regarded and treated as equal partners.

- Don't leave it too late to establish contact with parents. Starting early builds trust and their confidence in you.

- Ensure that you communicate positive news home as well as when things haven't gone well. Exclusively negative contact will be wearing for the parent and for you. Parents will be looking for signs of improvement, but will be unable to see them from home. Let them know.

- Be honest. Don't sugar the pill for parents. They want to know what's happening and what they can do to help.

- Listen to parents. I mean, really listen. Resist the urge to talk to start with and let them tell you what they need to – you'll learn a lot.

- Don't expect parents to sanction at home for issues at school. This is counter-productive.

- Be clear with parents about the support you need from them so that the child gets a clear, consistent message from all the adults and a strong sense that you are all working together on the same side – the side of the child.

- Parents have their own names – use them!

In all the behaviour training I have ever had (and what I have had can be summarised in a rather short leaflet written in a large font with a doodle at the end to cover the blank final page) parents weren't mentioned at all. Not once. After six years of headship in which the partnership we have forged with parents became one of our greatest accomplishments, I can now say with utter conviction that this is a glaring omission. Of course you can improve behaviour without involving parents, but it is likely to take longer, is more likely to fail and runs the risk of meeting resistance from parents if they are not involved in playing their part and supporting you to achieve the improvements you, and they, are looking for. If they are involved as equal partners I can assure you that any further problems that do come up, and they may well do, will be much easier to resolve because of the strength of the relationship, respect and trust that will have been built up in the past. This does not mean that it will be plain-sailing. You are working with parents in order to improve the behaviour of their child because it is causing concern. This will be a deeply emotional experience for them and this should be uppermost in our mind if we get emotional responses from parents.

Respect

I occasionally hear from teachers that parents these days lack the respect for teachers they once had, that some parents actively undermine them or some fail to support them when needed, such as with uniform, homework or attending detentions. Indeed, you can set your watch for the first week in September when at least one tabloid newspaper will run a major story on a teenager being placed in isolation for a week until their hair grows long enough so that the 'I H8 SKOOL' shaved into their skull is no longer visible. The newspaper will pitch the parent (my child is being denied their right to an education) against the Headteacher (we have rules in order for our school to run effectively), and once it gets as far as the front page of a national newspaper any relationship is well and truly on the rocks. This deterioration in respect over time may well be true; I don't know and, even if it is true, it's irrelevant. We work with the parents we have now and comparisons, favourable or otherwise, with the good old days when kids did as they were told and ADHD didn't exist, are pointless. Parents may well have similar opinions about us: in my first year as a Headteacher I had a mother walk into my office, look me straight in the eye and exclaim 'Things have gone right downhill since you took over at this school' and walk out. It remains one of the lowest points of my professional life and took some getting over. But get over it I did. It cannot have been easy for her to say that to me, so I had to take her feedback on the chin and use it to fuel my determination to improve as a Headteacher, and I'm really glad that I did. Any problems that do exist, and it is extremely rare for it to get to the tabloid stage or, like my situation above, can be addressed with good communication, an attitude that any issue is resolvable, and mutual respect. Request the support of your line manager if need be, that's what they're there for, but don't sub-contract contact with parents to your line manager on a permanent basis (a good line manager won't allow this anyway). I have supported colleagues with this in the past and can think of only one situation where tensions were such that I insisted that only I or another senior leader would communicate with the parents on an ongoing basis. Parents will respect you if you communicate well, communicate early and if they are convinced you are genuinely trying to improve the situation. If it sounds like parent-blaming or that you just want rid of their child you are cycling up a steep gradient into a headwind and you will never reach the summit. Afford parents the level of respect of an equal partner – that's what you need them to be and what they want to be too – and you won't go far wrong.

I have lost count of the number of parents who have reported to me that the quickest win a teacher could secure is to call them by their actual name. They are a person in their own right and, minor as this may sound, addressing someone as 'Austin's mum' instead of Mrs Mitchell can get you off on the wrong foot. You have probably had to go to the school's electronic administration system for the phone number you are after so the names of the parents are almost certainly going to be right next to that piece of information. It is always best to check as Austin's surname may well be Mitchell, but either or both parents may well have different surnames. If you don't have to resort to the school's admin system because the number is on Speed Dial #1 then you are probably already on first name terms with the parents anyway.

REFLECTION POINTS

- Think of an example when partnership with parents worked very successfully in improving the behaviour of one of your children. What do you put the success down to and how can you repeat this with other parents?

- Think of an example when partnership with parents was less effective in improving the behaviour of one of your children? Can you put your finger on why it wasn't as successful as you would have liked? And how can you ensure this isn't repeated?

Trust

Parents place their children in our care for seven or so hours a day, each day for 190 days a year. In some cases, such as the children who I have worked with who have complex medical conditions, the adults in the school need not only to teach their child but keep them alive too. There has to exist a basic level of trust from the parents that we are competent (see below) and, having seen this myself, relations can be very strained indeed if the parents do not feel that we are up to the job. Bryk and Schneider (2002)[1] describe trust in schools through four key elements: respect, competence, integrity and personal regard for others. I have already mentioned respect and competence. Integrity is a fundamental quality for adults choosing to work with children and we demonstrate it to parents through our actions that are consistent with our beliefs and with the ethos and principles of our schools. Personal regard is that thing that is at the heart of the best teachers – the things that they say and do that go beyond their job description. Interestingly, Bryk and Schneider also note that in schools characterised by high relational trust, the teachers and parents were more likely to collaborate on ways to work together for the benefit of the children educators and were, unsurprisingly at least to me, able to show marked gains in the learning of the children. By contrast, in schools where trust was considered to be less strong progress in reading and mathematics scores was slower.

Co-production

Working with parents is more than just telling them what's not working at school and what you're going to do about it. This is important, but if that is where the relationship ends then an opportunity has been missed. What you are aiming for is an agreement that you all have a role to play and clarity on what you are all going to do in order to improve the situation. I have a general preference that this is done with the full knowledge and presence of the child as they too have an obvious role in the process. I also have a preference that meetings are conducted in person. I know that this will not always be possible, but eye contact and the ability to read body language do help. I prefer to let parents do all the talking at the start of these meetings and force myself, as a keen talker, to listen intently, write lots of notes and let thoughts emerge in my head as to what we are going to do together. I am also keenly aware that schools can seem unwelcoming or intimidating places for some people, so this may prove an exception at least to start with. Clearly there is more that is likely to be done within school and therefore by school staff, and parents may well play a supportive role, but do not underestimate the power of this. We can be critical if we feel that parents do not support us or actively undermine us, so this is a chance to make it plain that their support is crucial and what form that support needs to take in order to secure improvements in their child's behaviour. It is at this point that the most pervasive mistake we make when working with parents usually occurs. This is the point when we ask parents to put in place consequences, sanctions or punishments at home for things that have happened at school. I am strongly of the opinion that this is not only wrong, but counter-productive, especially for the parents. Whatever happens in school needs to be dealt with in school. The parents can support from home in many ways, but extending consequences, sanctions or punishments into the home makes no sense. It is used to increase the amount of discomfort we want the child to experience and is fed by the logic that improvement in behaviour comes about by the simple application of power over the child by taking away the child's Xbox or phone, for example, for a period of time. It belongs in the same category as the pop behaviourism we encountered in Chapter 5 when looking at the use of rewards.

Having secured support from parents to help improve the behaviour of their child in school, it is vital that we then tell parents when things are improving. I stressed the importance in Chapter 5 of recognising progress. The parents are one step removed from the school so need to be explicitly told when things are getting better (they will be desperate to know, remember) and soon.

REFLECTION POINTS

- What are you trying to achieve by adding on punishments at home in addition to dealing with an issue within school?

- What can you ask parents to do in support from home to avoid them confiscating items or grounding their child as additional sanctions for school-based problems?

What could we need from parents?

Given that it is self-evident that working with parents is better than working without them, what is it that we may actually need from them to help improve the behaviour of their child? Let's also not forget what the parents may actually need from us too, and that is highlighted later on by Claire Ryan.

A clear, consistent message

There are times when you and parents may disagree, but ultimately you need them to support you publicly. A good example is a boy who joined us from a mainstream secondary school who would sometimes go home at the end of the day instead of staying a bit later to finish some work he should have completed during his lesson times. When that happened we called home and his mother simply drove him straight back to school. The message to him was crystal clear – these people are on the same side. Interestingly, he could have simply got off the bus early so that he could loiter and get in at 6pm. He knew that his mum ensured the work would be done somehow and that avoiding it would only make things worse.

Suggestions for successful strategies

The parents will know more about their child than we ever will, so we are fools if we don't take advantage of that. It doesn't mean that they are behaviour experts, indeed, they may be struggling with their child's behaviour at times outside of school too, but it does mean that their opinion is important and we must listen to them.

Setting time aside

I made my views clear earlier on parents not doubling up on punishment at home for something that has happened, and been dealt with, in school. We do need them to set time aside, though, to talk things through at home. In order to support us they need to know what we are trying to achieve and to know how things are going, which is why the onus is on us to communicate well in the first place. Reports can be good for this if done well. A report that is used in school to monitor behaviour in more detail, and to help the child keep track of how their day is going too, can be a good conversation centrepiece for home. Some schools use paper versions (which run the risk of never making it home or to Lesson 1), others are accessible to parents online. The parent can have a better conversation because they have some information to start from, rather than the limited 'So, how did today go?' It helps the parent if they are able to start it off with 'Maths seems like it was successful today. What was different compared to last lesson then?' We can advise them if necessary to start with successes rather than dive straight into 'Well, it looks like science was a disaster! What happened?'

REFLECTION POINTS

- What information do parents need from you in order to be able to support you well from home?
- How will they get the information in a timely manner and from whom?

A parent's point of view

Claire Ryan, a parent of a child with autism and a Parent Patron of the charity Ambitious About Autism, offers her own advice to teachers, having lived it herself:

> Remember many parents have had to fight for support and have seen their children fail. This doesn't make them 'difficult' or 'hard to reach'. It does mean trust might not be forthcoming without some creative thinking, time, patience and work. Some parents have never had positive home/school relationships before, but desperately want them. Breaking down those barriers takes trust, and for trust to develop, we need honesty and respect.

> Honesty is vital to build trust. Don't ever feel that saying 'I don't know' or 'I'm not the right person to help with that' makes you look unprofessional. Quite the opposite in fact. Knowing limitations and looking elsewhere for the right person to address issues is key to success.

> Always take parental concerns seriously and ask, 'What would you suggest?' 'What works at home?' 'How can we help?' 'What do you see as being the end goal?'

This advice is priceless and we would all do well to set our standards by it in all future work with parents.

Communication

There are three fundamentals for me with communication with parents:

1. Start early.
2. Ensure positive news gets home as well as negative.
3. Be honest.

I was certainly guilty of not getting in touch with parents early enough in some cases when I worked in a comprehensive. No wonder parents felt a sense of frustration that, if only I had contacted them sooner, something more could have been done to prevent things escalating. The overwhelming majority of readers will thankfully never have had to physically restrain a child in their professional lives, so it may shock you to know that if that does happen in a school there is no law that says the parent must be informed. This shock would pale into insignificance alongside the shock felt by a parent who learns at their annual consultation evening that their child has been restrained a number of times that year. This will also be true if you reveal to a parent at those annual meetings that things have not been good for a period of time. 'Why didn't you tell me sooner?' is likely to be their first very reasonable question to you. Looking back, the reason I didn't get in contact is largely because I rarely, if ever, spoke to or met with parents (see later regarding communication in secondary schools). This seems pathetic now, but it was the culture in which I worked and I didn't think deeply enough to realise that it was something that I should do more of. Leading on to my second point, when I eventually did need to make contact with parents it was inevitably to convey some bad news. This is why some parents learn to dread the phone ringing during the school day. We have worked really hard to ensure positivity in our communication with parents, yet it is still common for a parent to say, 'What's he done now?' as soon as I introduce myself on the phone or I pre-empt with 'Jarlath here; Lucas is fine by the way. Nothing to worry about.' It saddens me that I know that some parents need that immediate reassurance, so please bear in mind that, for some parents, contact from the school has been exclusively negative over the course of, in some cases, many years.

The amount of contact you have with parents is heavily dependent on a couple of major factors. Contact, especially face-to-face, between parents and staff in primary schools is likely to be far more common than between parents and staff in secondary schools and this can make a big difference. For obvious reasons many more parents are present at the school gate or on the playground at the start and end of the school day in primary schools. The teachers tend to be accessible at these times too, as many teachers walk out on to the playground with their classes. That makes these times natural opportunities for both parents and staff to talk things over regularly if needed. The other advantage in primary schools is that the child is likely to have one teacher, maybe two, so the relationship can be deeper and the parent can be reassured that the teacher knows their child really well. In secondary schools the vast majority of teachers may never see parents between annual parents' evening appointments and some not even then. Each child will also have upwards of 10 teachers a week, so the form tutor is likely to be the first point of contact, but they will have a harder job knowing how their tutees have been getting on all week. Distance, however, need not be the barrier it seems, as we all have multiple avenues of communication open to us.

My son is about to move schools and at a recent information evening we were informed that the planner was the way to communicate between school and home. I find this somewhat limiting for various reasons – there will be things that you (the teacher) or the parent wants to communicate that you don't want the child or other children reading; the boxes in planners provide very limited space; there is no guarantee the planner makes it to the right person; your child isn't taught by the teacher that needs to read it for another few days, and so on. I have always advocated in our school that staff and parents set up ways of communicating that work well for them. That is one of the main outcomes for our meet-the-tutor evening in the second week of the academic year. The parents and teacher work out what works best between themselves, so I see no reason as Headteacher to impose upon them one single way of communicating. This might be e-mail for one parent, for another it might be talking on the phone and for others it might be, if their child is on report, that they would like to see the report so that they can talk it through with their child each evening. Teachers are naturally concerned that this could become a free-for-all, but my experience shows that this is very rarely the case. I took the decision to place all our teachers' e-mail addresses on our website (many schools do the same) and braced myself for the deluge of e-mails to flow. It never happened. We found parents used e-mail very responsibly and it fitted in well with their own busy lives. My own e-mail address is obviously there too, so parents can go straight to me if they want. I did wonder if I would be inundated but, again, this never happened. Parents would contact me with good news or with news that they knew staff needed to know for the next day, such as the death of a pet, as they also knew that I would be plugged in to my e-mail in the evening.

One big no-no for me is when communication with a parent is used as a threat. 'I'll phone your mum if you carry on like that!' is a behaviourism glass hammer in your toolbox, but one I've heard many times. It is deployed when a teacher thinks that the threat, and it is a threat so let's not pretend it is anything but, will be enough to influence the child to improve their behaviour. The problem behind it is the implication that, if that improvement is forthcoming, the teacher won't tell the parent. If I am asked 'Are you going to call my mum?' my response is always the same – 'Yes. Your parents have a right to know how you're doing in school. I tell parents when things go well. I tell parents when things need to improve.'

How you go about communicating good news home to parents may well be influenced by your school policy. Some schools have postcards, usually designed by the children, on which you can write a quick note and the office will fill in the address details. The surprise of these landing on the doormat works really well, especially when the child doesn't know it's happening either, but, just like with praise in class, this can be overdone. If one arrives every couple of days for the most tenuous of reasons the effect wears off swiftly. Postcards, notes in planners and e-mail are nice, but I like nothing better than a phone call or, if the parent is at the gate at the end of the day, talking to the parent face-to-face. I can fit in far more in a two-minute conversation than I can in any postcard or e-mail. My other favourite is an e-mail of a photo or photos from a school event, a piece of work, a sports fixture or just capturing something in class. Schools take a lot of photos these days and we all have ways of storing them centrally so teachers can get access to them. A swift e-mail home with the photo attached and a 'Look what great things Seb has been getting up to today!' works wonders. Given that parents can't actually see what happens in school each day, photos are a little window into their children's lives between 9am and 3pm. This is so important if, like me, you work with children with communication difficulties who may not be able to explain what their day was like in any detail or if they are teenagers who respond with a 'Dunno' to any questions about their day in school. I know that the postcards can be kept as mementos, but remember that you can both send them home and make contact too. School policy or not, ensure that good news gets home somehow. We're a creative bunch and I know teachers come up with all sorts of ways to make this happen.

REFLECTION POINTS

- What is the balance between good and bad news that gets home? Does this need to be evened up? If so, how will this happen and who will do it?

- Are some parents considered hard-to-reach because the communication system is not flexible enough? How could this be addressed?

TAKING IT FURTHER – QUESTIONS AND ACTIVITIES FOR YOU AND YOUR COLLEAGUES

- Do we have enough flexibility in our communications with parents? What more could we do to improve contact with parents?

- Do we have some parents that we have labelled 'hard-to-reach'? What will we do to make it easier for them to reach us?

- Let's take a look at our culture – are we a school that goes all out to get good news home to parents? How do we do this?

- Do we ask parents to support us by, for example, confiscating devices at home as a result of things that have happened in school? What can we ask parents to do instead that will be more effective in supporting improvement?

Reference

1   Bryk, A.S. and Schneider, B. (2002) *Trust in Schools: A Core Resource for Improvement*. New York: Russell Sage Foundation.

9

WORKING IN PARTNERSHIP
WITH SUPPORT STAFF TO
IMPROVE BEHAVIOUR

Teamwork is not a preference, it is a requirement.

John Wooden

THE HEADLINES

- Teaching assistants (TAs) are the best assets we have in our classrooms to promote great behaviour.

- A culture of great behaviour is fostered best when teachers and TAs work well together as colleagues in the absence of a hierarchy. All adults are afforded the same respect by the children.

- TAs need good communication from teachers. Ensure they know:
  - your rules and expectations;
  - what you want them to do in response to poor behaviour;
  - what they can do without referring or deferring to you;
  - of any positive behaviour plans for specific children in your class and what they need to do to support that child or children.

- An agreed strategy in response to certain situations (also known as a script) helps teacher, TA and child by:
  - heading off 'ask mummy/ask daddy' approaches from children;
  - helping adults navigate stressful situations by relying on agreed verbal responses and other agreed actions;
  - making language concise and precise, thereby avoiding overloading the child with excessive language demands.

- Be humble enough to listen to TAs and ask their opinion. They will often have excellent ideas for improving behaviour and will be skilled at doing so themselves.

- Recognise that there may be times when dealing with behaviour when one of you needs to step away from a situation and the other colleague takes over.

- Teamwork to support behaviour improvement is less effective if only one of you ever works with a particular child. This can sometimes be the case for certain children with special educational needs who may spend a lot of their week with a member or members of support staff.

I have been a teacher for 17 years and I have seen the population of TAs grow very significantly in that time. When I first started teaching in a secondary school at the turn of the century more often than not I was on my own and I certainly had no training on working with TAs during my teacher training. My wife's experience was similar. She estimates a TA was in her primary class for about five hours a week. Nowadays in primary classes it seems there is a TA in the vast majority of classes for most, if not all, of the week. Less so in secondary schools, but the number has still risen considerably recently. Webster and Blatchford (2017)[1] note that 'The number of full-time equivalent TAs in mainstream schools in England has more than trebled since 2000, from 79,000 to 265,600 in 2016. In November 2016, TAs comprised 28% of the school workforce in England: 35% of the nursery and primary school workforce; 14% of the secondary school workforce; and 50% of the special school workforce.' Working with TAs deserves a book all to itself, and fortunately Webster et al. (2016)[2] have done just that with *Maximising the Impact of Teaching Assistants*. I am going to limit this chapter to working with TAs specifically to improve behaviour. TAs are your greatest assets – very poorly paid assets I'm sorry to say – and they often have great expertise. I liken them to the ravens of the Tower of London and without them our jobs would be far harder than they are already. I'm going to be very careful here because there are two major potholes to avoid. Firstly, it could be inferred that TAs are there to be deployed with the children whose behaviour we find hardest to manage. They aren't, but they are another adult or adults in your class so it is both unreasonable to expect them not to be involved in supporting the behaviour of the children they are working with and a wasted opportunity to work as a cohesive team if you insist that they aren't involved. Secondly, there is a danger that TAs are the *de facto* teachers for the children they are deployed to work with. By that I mean that the TA becomes the only adult that ever teaches the child. This sometimes happens gradually as the year progresses and the adults settle on a system whereby the teacher starts a lesson or activity and both the teacher and TA know, even if it has never been explicitly decided, that the TA's job is to listen intently and then work out how they will differentiate the task at hand for 'their' child (I use that language as I've met many a TA who has begun sentences with 'My statement …' or 'My child …' indicating a sense of ownership). The child is in on the game too as they know that they don't need to listen to the teacher – they will get their instructions from the TA once the teacher has stopped talking. They may even leave the room for their work, so may be busy getting their gear together.

Drip, drip, drip, nip

Another adult or adults in your classroom have the opportunity to constantly reinforce your expectations of the children you are all working with, constantly recognise great behaviour and constantly nip tiny things in the bud before they escalate. All of the advice to come in this chapter is secondary to the incessant reinforcement and support a TA can give you in terms of what you want from your class. I will mention again later how important it is for TAs to know your rules and expectations because, without that, they can't support you as effectively. Once all the adults in your room are clear about what is and is not acceptable they are able to set about helping the children to meet those expectations. That means that the following kind of comments will happen without your prompting and, maybe, without you even hearing.

- 'Let's have your homework out on the desk ready to hand in before Mr O'Brien asks for it.'
- 'Sort your tie out before you walk in the door, Darren.'
- 'Superb responses to those questions, Alisha.'
- 'Yesterday's maths lesson was superb, Jody. More of the same today, please.'
- 'I'm sending a Good News postcard home for your behaviour in today's lesson, Danielle.'
- 'Remind me what the rule is about talking whilst working, Dia. That's right, so let's stop talking and get on, please.'
- 'Show me that you've recorded your homework in your planner, Leanne, as I know you didn't write it in there last week and forgot to complete it.'

Tiny things get sorted, sometimes without your knowledge; they don't escalate and things run a lot more smoothly. Conversely, without that team approach you are the one sorting out all of the issues and, as happened to me when I was a student teacher, the TA sits there, arms crossed, shaking their head at your inability to cope.

Given that low-level disruption is reported as a one of the biggest behavioural concerns teachers, parents and Ofsted have,[3] the effectiveness of the support of other adults in your classroom can go a long way to reducing or eradicating this as a problem.

Teamwork

TAs will be in your class for a reason. Perhaps you have a class TA (as in many primary classrooms) whom you deploy as you see fit from lesson to lesson or activity to activity. Perhaps some TAs are assigned to work with specific children because of their special educational needs, be they medical, learning or behavioural needs (or some combination of all three), which means in a secondary environment that the TA or TAs in your class may change every lesson or so. However your staffing is arranged, you are a team for the time you spend together and it is in everyone's best interests that this team works as well as possible. Clearly a teacher and class TA in a primary classroom can build up a strong relationship over time such that in the best classrooms their routines, scripts and responses to poor behaviour, and their preventative work to stop it happening in the first place, can become almost automatic. In these highly effective teams, too, there is no hierarchy of authority with the children. There is no 'You're in trouble with Mrs Shaw now. I'm going to get her to come and deal with you,' from the TA. All adults are afforded the same respect and the children respond to all the adults in the same way. I know that this lack of an obvious hierarchy is not universally liked by some teachers I have spoken to about this, but for me this appeal to authority is a weak position. It is no different to 'Go and see the Headteacher!' from the class teacher and conveys both a sense from the teacher that they've run out of ideas and that seniority has a magical effect on improving behaviour – it doesn't.

Cohesion between adults in the classroom doesn't happen by accident and comes about by strong communication between the adults, high levels of mutual trust and respect and by spot coaching, mentoring and training along the way. (Coaching and mentoring works both ways, by the way. I've been taught plenty by exceptional members of support staff, so be humble enough to know that you can learn a lot from your support staff colleagues.) This ability to build strong partnerships is less straightforward in a secondary environment where you may only work with a particular TA for as little as one hour a fortnight. It will take a lot longer but is still an aim well worth aspiring to. In the sections to follow I will cover what I see as the main areas to ensure your working relationship with TAs contributes to the best possible behaviour in your lessons.

Communication

TAs are not mind-readers, but ask one and they'll tell you that, with some teachers, they spend a lot of time guessing what the teacher wants because they simply haven't been told. They can't support us and do their job well if this is the case. Don't let this happen to you.

REFLECTION POINTS

Before we go any further, ensure you can answer yes to the following questions:

- Do the TAs you work with:
  - know the rules and expectations in your class?
  - know what you expect of them in response to poor behaviour?
  - know your level of delegation (i.e. can they award merits or your equivalent, or can they give warnings or your equivalent for poor behaviour)?
  - know the agreed actions of any positive behaviour plans for specific children in your class?

If the answer to any of those questions is no then consider how you will address them so that TAs can be more effective in supporting behaviour in your classroom. Without this basic knowledge the TAs will be dependent on you, disempowering them and increasing your workload, or they may unintentionally contradict or undermine you when dealing with situations themselves.

Whichever way you mutually prefer to communicate is less important than the fact that it happens at all. When I worked in a special school teaching children with severe and profound and multiple learning difficulties it was common to have a class of nine children of secondary age with between three and six TAs. We established a way of communicating at the start of each lesson because it wasn't feasible to meet beforehand. I would talk directly to the children, but the TAs also knew that everything I wanted from them was contained within that message. It avoided a duplication of effort and the lessons started swiftly with no dead time. Some teams prefer lesson plans, others work the way I did above and others meet at the start of every day to plan ahead. Find what works for you, but if there is no plan then you will end up having a 10-second snatched conversation after the lesson has started or rely on the TA to guess what's in your head, neither of which is ideal.

Capturing progress

TAs pick up a lot of useful information in lessons and will see things that we may well miss, but without a system to capture this much of it will be lost.

If you have specific children on a positive behaviour plan, or your equivalent, TAs are able to add information as to how that child is progressing. Post-It notes, annotating a copy of the behaviour plan or access to your online behaviour tracking database via a tablet all work well here. Relying on memory at the end of the week, half-term or term do not work well. Care does needs to be taken when recording or capturing information during the course of a lesson to ensure information such as a child's behaviour plan or their page on your tracking system is not left lying around or is visible to other children.

Scripts and agreed responses

We mentioned the use of scripts in Chapter 7 on restorative conversations. I like using scripts (agreed behaviours and responses from adults) in certain situations and working in partnership with other adults is one of them. Scripts can help here for three main reasons:

1. They can help take some of the heat out of difficult situations for the adults (and for the children) by relying on agreed responses. This can reduce the stress brought on by thinking 'what on Earth am I going to do now?' whilst things are happening around you. For example, you may have a planned response, known too by your TA(s) remember, to a particular behaviour from a specific child. Let's say this child sometimes responds to being asked to start some work by refusing – 'I'm not doing it!' Maybe the page is ripped out of the exercise book or the book and the child's pencil case end up on the floor. These are the kinds of situations that can escalate very quickly but remember our first job is to ensure we de-escalate situations – our version of the medical profession's Hippocratic 'First, do no harm'. They can escalate quickly because we can dive straight in with an emotional response, sometimes an unenforceable one, such as 'You will do it! I'll make you!' and so the desire to win and an inevitable stand-off begins. If you want to win, the child has to lose and they probably won't want to lose, especially in full view and earshot of their classmates. 'I'll leave you to gather your things and one of us [leaving this open-ended helps as a change of face (see below) can work here] will be back to see if you need any help in two minutes' might work as a script. The TA or you get to break the stand-off and give the child a chance to save some face. I've seen work avoidance as a common behaviour from children that have joined our school after having to leave a mainstream secondary, normally because of their behaviour. They have become sure that much of what school demands from them

(and not just in terms of work) will be unachievable so it is safer to avoid situations and tasks than it is to fail (recall Chapter 1 and the message we need to convey to children that we're here to catch them, not catch them out). Maybe that script works first time, maybe it doesn't. You can tell from afar and then leave them alone if they're working, check in with them with a thumbs up from the other side of the room or, if they are still to start work your script can continue. A change of face might be an option here where the other member of staff can take over if you think that will help – 'Here's what you need to do to get started,' for example, or a success reminder such as 'These sums are set out the same way as yesterday, and your work there was brilliant. Look back one page to see how you did it.'

2. They significantly reduce the amount of language being used. If a child is in a heightened state of emotion (and you may be too) their ability to listen intently is reduced. Rattling off a series of instructions or demands will be ineffective. Limiting instructions calmly but firmly to what you want first of all – 'Sit down, please' – instead of a stream of 'If you don't sit down, get your book out, hand in your homework, write me a letter of apology and start work right now I'll get the Headteacher, put you in isolation and call your mum,' is more likely to work. The child is less likely to remember the list you just gave them and is more likely to remember the threats, partly because they are threats but also because they were the last things he or she heard. I was once kicked in the testicles and spat at in the face by a child in a corridor between lessons and a TA, undoubtedly trying to help, tried to take over by shouting a stream of demands and threats at the child. The child was in crisis (children don't do those kinds of things for fun) and quite clearly couldn't process what was being said (shouted). 'Let's just get James into this empty classroom. He can't hear you, Debbie,' I had to tell her. And to James I kept it simple: 'We need to sit in here, James.' Anything more than that was too much for most of us to process in a serious situation, especially after a direct hit in the testicles.

3. The other main advantage to scripts when working with other colleagues is that it prevents the 'ask mummy, ask daddy' tactic from being successful. Those of us who are parents are well used to this – if a child doesn't get the answer they want from one parent, they may seek to get it from the other and sometimes this works well. If successful, this evolves in the long run into the child working out who is more likely to accede to their request and they will go straight there from then on, reducing the chances of being turned down. You may work with a child who requests to go to the toilet numerous times each lesson and you suspect that work avoidance may be involved. (This is an issue fraught

with pitfalls. The first school I worked in resorted to locking all toilets during lesson times and a member of staff ended up with a teenager wetting themselves in her lesson as a result. The fallout was big.) Knowing that the same answer, exactly the same answer, will be forthcoming from whomever the child asks immediately neutralises this as an approach for a child. The added bonus is that this reinforces the lack of a hierarchy. The adults in the room are a team, who expect the same and respond in the same way.

Scripts are not reserved for situations when you are working with other colleagues. They can be successfully deployed when working by yourself too.

Change of face

I mentioned earlier something called a 'change of face'. Have you ever found yourself in a situation with a child where you thought that your presence could be contributing to the problem? I have, but it is not easy to admit, especially in the heat of the moment. Our determination and tenacity to see something through, our professional pride or our ego sometimes prevents us from recognising that a situation may resolve itself more swiftly if another adult were to come along and support or take over, yet this may be precisely what the situation needs. We worry that we may appear weak or that to bow out and ask a TA to step in will result in a loss of authority. On the contrary, I see it as a sign of professional security when someone recognises that a situation can be resolved in such a way. This can be a successful way of defusing a situation if an adult has become the focus of a child's ire as, despite still being upset or angry, the child may see the new adult as helping to make things better as opposed to the person who, in their eyes, caused the problem in the first place. When I have recognised in myself the need to step away I have simply asked a TA something like 'could you work with Alice for the next 10 minutes please?' Because the TA has been in the lesson with me from the start they know full well what's going on, but the language is deliberately low-key to prevent this kind of approach: 'Alice isn't doing a thing that I say! Mr Short, let's see if you can have more luck!'

I was once asked to support Damien, who was perched atop an eight-foot brick wall at the edge of our school boundary, one afternoon. 'I'm the reason Damien is there,' I had to say to a very disappointed member of staff. 'Me turning up will only make this situation worse.' I arranged for a colleague to support, but it took some explaining to the member of staff, who didn't know the full story, that nothing good would come of me being there.

When you don't recognise in yourself the need to step away, or you see that it's not working for a TA and you feel that you should support by taking over, this can be more problematic. Some schools, my own included, have an agreed script for just such a situation. Ours is taken from a training provider we use and has two parts: 'Help is available,' says one member of staff to the other, indicating that they think a change of face will help. The member of staff dealing with the situation may disagree, but if a short time later the supporting member of staff is clear that a change is needed the script becomes 'More help is available'. This is a clear instruction that one member of staff is going to step in and relieve the original member of staff – remember there is no hierarchy here so a TA may say this to the Headteacher. They may still fundamentally disagree but we, as a team, agreed that we will step away and discuss this issue later as, obviously, this is no time or place to argue about the finer points of a colleague's decision-making. It is a rare thing indeed – I've never actually got as far as 'More help is available' either as a recipient or provider of support, but knowing that the routine is there is helpful and 'Help is available' is a good prompt to reassess how things are going.

Dependency

Working together as a team with TAs to improve behaviour can also help prevent a dependency building up between an adult and child. By that I mean that the child spends so much time with a member of support staff that, in words I've heard more than once, 'I only work with Mrs Chapman!', or more worryingly but still a possibility, a TA says 'He'll only behave for me' or 'I'm the only one that can get him to calm down when he gets like this'. One of my major concerns in our schools in general, and this is well outside of the scope of this book, is the amount of time that children with special educational needs spend being taught almost exclusively by TAs, so you can see if teachers spend little or no time working directly with some children in their class, it follows that they are less well placed to support that child's behaviour if things get tricky.

REFLECTION POINT

- Estimate the proportion of the week (in primary) or of your lessons (in secondary) that children who receive support from TAs are actually taught by you and the proportion they are taught by TAs. Do you need to redress the balance here? If so, how are you going to do that?

Working with new staff

There was a period after about four years of being a Headteacher where I had that dangerously satisfying feeling when I thought that we'd broken the back of behaviour problems in our school. The feeling didn't last long and not for the reason you're probably thinking of. It wasn't because behaviour started to nosedive; far from it. In many ways it had never been better, but we went through some staff changes and I realised one really important fact. Staff new to your school will not simply absorb your ethos, your expectations and your thinking by osmosis. I had forgotten that some colleagues hadn't been on the journey with us, so hadn't lived through some of the tough times, and they surely were tough. A colleague, Karen, who had been at the school long before I arrived summed it up perfectly, 'We grew up together'. Yes, we had an induction for new staff, but that small amount of training, both in terms of time and content, could only really scratch the surface. I failed to realise that induction and ongoing training needed to be deeper and really hammer home the fine details of both the policy and underlying principles of the school's approach to behaviour. Given how long it took me to get to the position I am in now in terms of knowledge, skills and experience, it is negligent of me to simply expect new colleagues to attend a one-hour induction session and then be match fit.

Bear this in mind when a new member of staff joins your class. They may be highly experienced, but new to your school, or it may be the first day that they have ever worked in a school. Obviously you have little or no space for formal training during the school day, but you can spot-coach and mentor newer colleagues in the midst of lessons. This can be powerful: it's immediate, short and focused. You have to give due consideration to the fact that you have 30 pairs of ears nearby so need to keep the conversation discreet and professional, but I find it far more effective than discussing a situation after the lesson or after school, when the moment is lost.

TAKING IT FURTHER – QUESTIONS AND ACTIVITIES FOR YOU AND YOUR COLLEAGUES

- Let's take a fresh look at the induction programme for our TAs. (You do have an induction programme for your TAs don't you? I'm always amazed at schools that offer TAs no initial training whatsoever.) What training do we provide on behaviour? Is this sufficient? If not, what needs to be included?

- Following on from this, do we ensure that our TAs are full participants in our INSET and CPD programme for behaviour? It is unreasonable to expect these colleagues to be as effective as teachers in supporting behaviour if they don't receive as much, or any, training.

- Do we have a hierarchy in our classrooms and in our school? Could we empower TAs to contribute more to a culture of great behaviour? For example, could they award merits/bonuses/points or send postcards home?

- How do we gather information from TAs when we gauge improvements in positive behaviour plans?

References

1   Webster, R. and Blatchford, P. (2017) *The Special Educational Needs in Secondary Education (SENSE) Study. Final Report: A Study of the Teaching and Support Experienced by Pupils with Statements and Education, Health and Care Plans in Mainstream and Special Schools.* University College London Institute of Education. http://maximisingtas.co.uk/assets/content/sense-final-report.pdf (accessed 11 December 2017).

2   Webster, R., Russell, A. and Blatchford, P. (2016) *Maximising the Impact of Teaching Assistants: Guidance for School Leaders and Teachers.* Abingdon: Routledge.

3   Ofsted (2014) *Below the Radar: Low-Level Disruption in the Country's Classrooms.* Reference no. 140157. September 2014. www.gov.uk/government/uploads/system/uploads/attachment_data/file/379249/Below_20the_20 radar_20-_20low-level_20disruption_20in_20the_20country_E2_80_99s_20classrooms.pdf (accessed 11 December 2017).

10

SPECIAL EDUCATIONAL NEEDS AND BEHAVIOUR

Some of those who are frightened of people with intellectual disabilities may never have met anyone with disabilities. [This is] based on a great fear of change; people do not want to be disturbed in their security or have their values system questioned. They do not want to open their hearts to those who are different.

Jean Vanier, *Becoming Human*

THE HEADLINES

- Children with special educational needs are not predisposed to poorer behaviour than their peers.

- Schools and classrooms can be difficult places for them to learn if their needs are not well met and this can heavily influence their behaviour.

- Do not be seduced by labels, be informed by them. There is no one single way to teach all children with autism any more than there is one single way to teach girls.

- Become best friends with your schools Special Educational Needs Coordinator (SENCo). They can provide advice, coaching, support and training, or they will know someone who can.

- Punishments and sanctions for poor behaviour are likely to be ineffective if behaviour has resulted from a child's needs going unsupported.

- The Equality Act 2010 requires schools to make reasonable adjustments for children with special educational needs.

- Recommended support strategies for many issues are remarkably, and helpfully, similar:
  - use clear, concise language;
  - positive, explicit expectations and rules;
  - get children to repeat back instructions and expectations;
  - provide structure and routine;
  - use visual support to break up complex tasks;
  - provide regular developmental feedback.

I wanted to dedicate a chapter solely to the subject of special educational needs and disabilities (SEND) and behaviour for two main reasons. Firstly, I see the terms *SEND* and *behaviour* used interchangeably (and wrongly) all the time. There is a tendency in our profession to expect that children with special needs are more likely to be predisposed to behaving poorly. They aren't, but the statistics I detail below will make it plain to you why this myth is out there. The real reasons – that they are less likely to have their needs met (refer back to Chapter 2 and how negative behaviour communicates an unmet need), and that they may find it more difficult to do well in our schools as defined narrowly and restrictively by exams and grades (remember Ross Greene's 'kids will do well if they can' mantra) – are unfortunately not well understood and are, indeed, rejected as teacher-blaming by some. The second reason is linked to the first; if more teachers understood how they could better meet the needs of the children they teach who have special educational needs then incidents of poor behaviour would reduce significantly to the benefit of everyone.

The lie of the land

The latest annual figures from England's Department for Education on both permanent exclusion (a child is expelled and cannot return to that school) and fixed-term exclusion (a child is suspended from attending a school for a defined period of time) make concerning reading, and not just in terms of children with SEND.[1] They note that both permanent and fixed-term exclusions rose in the last two years, bucking a downward trend in previous years. The picture for children with special educational needs is dire:

- Pupils with identified special educational needs (SEN) accounted for *almost half* of all permanent exclusions and fixed period exclusions.
- Pupils with SEN support had the highest permanent exclusion rate and were *almost 7 times more likely* to receive a permanent exclusion than pupils with no SEN.
- Pupils with an Education, Health and Care (EHC) plan or with a statement of SEN had the highest fixed period exclusion rate and were *almost six times more likely* to receive a fixed period exclusion than pupils with no SEN.

I cannot see how anyone can fail to be shocked and saddened by those three statistics. I hope that you can see why I contend above that it would be only too easy to arrive at the view that children with SEND must therefore be more predisposed to poor behaviour. Fixed-term and permanent exclusion are, hopefully, at the extreme end of the sanctions spectrum, so I am going to stick my neck out here and bet that children with SEND will also be grossly over-represented in detentions, time spent in isolation rooms in secondary schools, time spent sat outside the Headteacher's office and any other sanction you care to name that we don't have nationwide data for. It is worth noting at this point that, for the last period statistics were available for separate Ofsted judgements of behaviour, a far greater proportion of special schools were judged to be outstanding for behaviour (54%) compared to all other schools (33%).[2] The reasons for their superior performance in behaviour terms as suggested by those inspection outcomes are, in my experience, contained within this book. Staff working in special schools often develop a deep understanding of behaviour and, given the complexity of needs they support, are clear that unmet needs lead to poorer behaviour.

A health warning

There is one major hazard to avoid when talking about special educational needs and behaviour and that is the seductiveness of the label – I want to make it clear that there isn't one single way to work with children with, say, ADHD or autism or Down syndrome (they are sometimes comorbid, and I once taught a girl with all three conditions) – indeed, any attempt to do so is doomed to failure. My aim is to make it plain to you how you can best support children with these conditions and how those conditions may manifest themselves in your classroom (may is the operative word there as, for example, not all children with autism will have a sensory integration problem). Not all children with the same diagnosis or diagnoses behave in the same way. You can, though, if you don't take account of their needs, exacerbate a situation. This is where problems arise and this is why children with SEND are grossly over-represented in the behaviour statistics.

REFLECTION POINT

- Take a closer look at the children who always seem to be in detention or who persistently fall foul of the behaviour system in other ways. Are children with special needs over-represented here? If so, what could be done to support their needs better so that things don't get to the sanctions stage as often?

Speech, language and communication needs (SLCN)

Speech, language and communication needs (SLCN) are far, far more than just children having trouble talking. Consider for a moment just *some* of the skills that are required to communicate effectively:

- Producing speech that others can understand.
- Putting the correct words together into coherent sentences and longer constructions.
- An effective working memory (see later on in this chapter for more on this) so that you can listen to others, understand what they are saying and plan what you are going to say in return.
- An understanding of idioms ('Jarlath, you're full of beans today!').
- Managing the social norms of communication.

Many of the children I work with have difficulties in one or more of these areas, but may well have strengths in others. For example, some are very articulate and can talk all day long in a very coherent manner on a subject of their choice. They understand many of the social norms of communication and will wait patiently for the other person in the conversation to finish talking. However, they haven't really been listening as their working memory can't keep up or is full holding what they will say next. I remember one conversation in our Sixth Form when one student was talking to another, who appeared to be listening intently, about Doctor Who. The other student was simply waiting for them to finish so they could talk about The Simpsons. From afar it looked like an in-depth conversation, but it was simply two people talking about their favourite things, neither really listening to the other at all.

Teachers who work in Early Years know only too well that young children who struggle to communicate and make themselves understood can become frustrated and behave poorly as a result. They know this because it is extremely common – all young children are developing both their communication skills and their emotional self-regulation – and these teachers are therefore well skilled in explicitly teaching communication skills and good habits of self-regulation. The older children get the more likely speech, language and communication difficulties are to be missed and regarded as behavioural difficulties. Primarily this is because the behaviour is overt and the unmet need may be covert. The behaviour is in your face, sometimes literally, and that dominates your attention with the cause potentially remaining hidden. I liken this to concentrating on a rash but not realising that it is the result of an invisible, and as yet undiagnosed, virus (there is good evidence that communication difficulties are often unrecognised[3]). For instance, Gregory and Bryan (2009) found that young people without speech, language and communication needs persevered with tasks they found difficult or asked for help, but those with such needs rarely admitted that they had not understood or needed help; instead, they simply gave up.[4] Studies have shown that children with speech, language and communication needs are more likely to develop behavioural, emotional and social difficulties (BESD) than typically developing children, with prevalence rates as high as 35–50%.[5,6,7]

Table 10.1 Ways you can help children whose behaviour may indicate a speech, language and communication difficulty

Look out for ...	You can help by ...
Children not carrying out your instructions	Checking they understand your instructions. Can they repeat it back to you?
Children not appearing to listen	Ensuring they understand your language. Explicitly teach core and complex vocabulary*
Children who struggle to tell you why they did something	Supporting them with the vocabulary needed to explain their feelings and actions and to put a chronology together
Children who appear rude by interrupting or by making other social mistakes	Teaching and modelling the appropriate social norms around communication
Children who give up	Check they understand what was required in the first place

* Speech and language therapists will always recommend pre-teaching new core vocabulary. For example, if you are taking on a new topic it may be helpful for children to know some of the key terms they may be encountering for the first time. *Magma, subduction, tectonic, epicentre* and *seismologist* are fascinating and beautiful words but may be baffling to a child who has no idea what you are talking about and this can get in the way of the joy of learning about the fascinating subject of volcanoes and earthquakes.

REFLECTION POINTS

- Consider the language needs of the children you are working with when asking them to talk about their feelings or when undertaking restorative justice work.

- Avoid repeating instructions or questions where you rephrase each time – you may well know that you are asking the same thing, but the child may consider them to be entirely separate questions and be frustrated at a stream of questions they have no time to answer. 'What is 4^2?' and 'What is 4 x 4?' are effectively the same question, but may not seem so to some children.

- The same is true of instructions regarding behaviour. Rephrasing is likely to be unhelpful (unless you've been too verbose or used language they can't understand in the first place). Keeping the instructions concise and simple is *always* the way to go.

Attention Deficit Hyperactivity Disorder (ADHD)

Without doubt the most maligned and misrepresented condition I know, ADHD is the poor, illegitimate cousin of the SEND world. Misrepresented and maligned because of the lazy stereotype that it is simply feral children high on sugar who won't behave, with feckless parents who can't control them.

Attention deficit hyperactivity disorder (ADHD) is actually a neurodevelopmental disorder that amounts to a group of behavioural symptoms that can include inattentiveness, hyperactivity and acting impulsively. It is immediately obvious why schools and classrooms can present challenges at times to children with ADHD given the clear need to maintain attention for long periods, self-regulate levels of activity and to control impulses in a highly social, highly structured environment. The good news is that there is much that we can do to help children with this condition manage the demands of the school environment to their, and everyone else's, best advantage.

It is worth knowing that approximately 60–80% of children with ADHD will have at least one other condition such as a speech, language and communication need (see above), or a literacy or motor difficulty[8] and, as a result, much good practice in this area is likely to be effective in supporting other children who do not have ADHD.

Ways you can help your children with ADHD

- Accept that it is a real issue for that child and that it is simply not a naughty child determined to ruin your lesson.
- Have rules and expectations that are clear and unambiguous and written in a positive way detailing what you do want rather than what you don't want. For example, *We walk in the corridors* as opposed to *Don't run in the corridors*, or *We listen in silence when someone else is talking* as opposed to *Don't interrupt the teacher*. This may sound minor, but *Don't run in the corridors* doesn't preclude hopping, crawling or moonwalking whereas *We walk in the corridors* is clear about what you do expect. Likewise *We listen in silence . . .* is clear whereas *Don't interrupt the teacher* is ambiguous – a child can interrupt others or use the justification that, although they were talking, they didn't feel that it amounted to interrupting.
- Know that children with ADHD are more likely to have issues with dyspraxia (an impairment of the organisation of movement). You may see this in handwriting problems and can support this by knowing when typing or the use of dictation software are smart substitutes for handwriting. I don't advocate removing the need to write by hand entirely, but there will be times when the brain is working far faster than the hand can keep up and this can impede progress, such as when they have a great story brewing but the plot slips out of their working

memory because they can't get it down on paper quickly enough. When they are handwriting they can be further supported with the use of pencil grips, writing slopes and/or footstools. (I had been a teacher for seven years before an occupational therapist taught me how important posture is to handwriting.)

- Make longer tasks into a series of smaller ones (known in the business as chunking). In order to prevent a build-up of dependency ('What do I do next, miss?' every 30 seconds) use a visual schedule such as *First – Next – Last* or *Now – Next* strips. These are a bit like comic strips with each step made very clear on them. They can be in text or in pictures, or both. This works well, for example, in science experiments and recipes in cooking are presented like this already, but you can reduce the literacy (and numeracy) complexity in this way if you need to. For example, you can instruct the child to add two cups of flour instead of 100 grams of flour if measuring 100 grams accurately is currently a step too far. Clearly you still want to work towards working in grams, but measuring in a simpler unit can help independence in the short term. (Chunking was a very successful teaching strategy when I learned to row. The coaches deconstructed the entire rowing stroke and broke it down into small bits. I learned each one and then learned how to put them all together smoothly, as we may have done when we teach our own children to tie shoelaces.)

- Help the child understand when something is finished, or what a successful piece of work actually looks like. This, along with chunking, can really help children navigate their way through a piece of work and know when to stop.

- Regular feedback and reinforcement are crucial. This doesn't mean going overboard on the praise – this is usually ineffective – it means drip-feeding advice as tasks progress. There is a danger of contradicting myself here with the advice above about independence, but the difference here is that they are not dependent on you to know what to do next.

- Check that the child has a good understanding both of the work they are to complete and the behaviour that is expected of them. Get them to repeat back and make sure you or another member of staff recognises when they have achieved their goal. Checking behaviour expectations may sound unnecessary, but remember that there are subtle differences, and sometimes not so subtle differences, in what we expect or allow depending on the nature of the subject or activity. A school will have a constant set of rules, but what happens in the drama studio, on the school playing field, the science lab, the food technology kitchen, the art room and the design technology workshop will be different. Acceptable noise levels or rules for uniform such as having hair tied back in the DT workshop or shoes off in the drama studio to name just two may change depending on the location and this will be as true for primary schools as it is for secondary schools.

- Understand that there are potential pitfalls with timed tests. This obviously doesn't mean that you should avoid them, but understand that issues such as handwriting pace (mentioned earlier) can cause problems where speed is important, so consider access arrangements such as the use of a computer to type instead.

- Use success reminders – when things went well in the past and, crucially, why they went well. 'Your last poetry reading was really good because you practised in the hall a few times, went over the tricky words at home, made sure your voice reached the back of the hall and slowed down.'

- Appreciate how hyperactivity may manifest itself in that child and what you can do to help them. Look at their seating position both in terms of their posture and where they sit in the classroom. Do they need a pencil grip and/or a footstool and/or a writing slope?

- Appreciate how inattentiveness may manifest itself in that child. Just because a child is not looking directly at you it does not mean that their attention is elsewhere. Do you really need to insist on eye contact? This may well be very intimidating for that child and, counter-productively, lead to reduced attention. Check that they are listening by asking them to repeat back what they need to do. Where they sit can heavily influence their attentiveness too. Are they seated at the back by the window that looks out on to the playing field? I recently chaired an annual review for a Year 8 student, Ryan, who has both ADHD and a language difficulty. He was sat facing my office window which looks out on to some beautiful woodland. As he was talking he seamlessly and imperceptibly shifted from talking about maths, his favourite subject, to the squirrel that was scampering up the tree outside the window.

- Appreciate how impulsivity can manifest itself in that child. You may be irritated by constant interruptions and consider this intensely rude, or the child may appear reckless in their behaviour or struggles to wait their turn. Anything that can help the child press the pause button for a short period will help here. Talk tokens, for example, have been effective for us with some students who constantly ask questions (and also, interestingly, for those who ask none). The child hands the teacher the talk token before they ask their question and stretches out the moment, helping them manage their impulses.

REFLECTION POINTS

Plan for success with a child or children with ADHD by giving some deep thought to, and revisiting regularly, the following questions:

- Where and when is this child hyperactive?

- What does this look like?

- Where and when is this child (and us) already managing this well?

- What is currently effective in helping this child manage this well? (See above.)

- What will it take to extend this to those times where they (and us) are not managing as well?

- Ask the same questions, but replace 'hyperactive' with 'inattentive and impulsive'.

Autism

'Can you write the date please?' I asked Jacob at the start of our Year 9 physics lesson. Two minutes later I looked at his exercise book and he had beautifully written 'The date please' complete with underlining and, as I wrongly assumed at the time, a smug look on his face. I considered it a provocation, but a member of support staff seated next to him sensed my irritation and expertly deflected me away, educating me after the lesson that Jacob had genuinely carried out my instruction to the letter. Jacob has autism and, naïve mainstream teacher that I was then, I knew no better and did not understand him at all. If ADHD is the poor SEND cousin, then autism is the misunderstood one. Misunderstood because it is common to hear assumptions that all people with autism have obsessions, are devoid of empathy and are quirky.

Autism is a developmental disability that cannot be cured (nor would many people with autism actually want it to be cured) and is a spectrum condition, which means that, although there are common difficulties, individual children will be affected in different ways. The National Autistic Society (NAS) states that children with autism will have 'persistent difficulties with social communication and social interaction and restricted and repetitive patterns of behaviours, activities or interests since early childhood, to the extent that these limit and impair everyday functioning'.[9] It is important to know that a proportion of people with autism will also have a learning difficulty and/or other conditions such as ADHD.

Ways you can help your children with social communication difficulties

- Appreciate that children with autism may find the subtleties and nuances of communication such as body language difficult to interpret. Jacob's literal interpretation of my instruction is a good example. They may miss or misinterpret the meaning in your raised eyebrows (teachers are expert eyebrow-users remember), the look on your face or your tone of voice. This works both ways as Jacob and I demonstrated earlier. I misread him too and this is known as the double empathy problem.
- Stick to clear, concise language. They may be confused by attempts at sarcasm, exaggeration such as 'I've told you a million times!' or the use of idioms such as 'It's raining cats and dogs out there' (our speech and language therapists and teachers explicitly teach our students the real meaning behind idioms and when you stop to consider how many we use in everyday life you will see why). I recall once explaining to a visiting prospective parent that our Sixth Formers had just returned from a week in Paris and asked Leo to join the discussion as he was passing and had been on the trip. 'It's tough being in the Sixth Form, eh Leo?' I said, to which he replied quizzically, 'What's tough about being in the Sixth Form, Jarlath?' I had tried to be funny and this was completely lost on Leo. Responding to a child's request for help with 'Wait a minute' means one thing to you, but something very precise to someone else if you are not back in 60 seconds.
- Offer alternative means of communication, especially at times of higher stress, such as the use of symbols or written schedules. There are many ways of doing this: a child may feel embarrassed to ask to go to the toilet and you insisting on them asking verbally may well increase anxiety further. Likewise, a card with a picture of a toilet or toilet symbol on it may still be unsatisfactory as the need is advertised to others who can see it. A simple square of an agreed colour, for example, communicates quickly and easily to you what is needed without a loss of dignity.

Ways you can help your children with social interaction difficulties

This is the area of difficulty that can lead to children with autism being labelled as quirky or appearing to lack empathy. Just because what you perceive to be the right words and actions are not forthcoming from the child does not mean they don't care for others.

- Accept that some children may prefer their own company and try not to force them to play or work with others. There is a difference between wanting to socially interact, but not knowing how, and wanting to be on your own. Previous adverse experiences may linger in the memory too, resulting in an understandable reluctance for that to happen again. They could also be exhausted and stressed from socialising with others and need more time out than others.
- Recognise that seeking the company of a select few children, or one specific child, could be because they are familiar and therefore more predictable. This predictability could also be why adult company may be preferred over that of other children.
- Shared interests, which can be focused and intense for people with autism, are a good place to start with encouraging social interaction as there is some existing common ground.
- Work on how to start and finish conversations. This may sound unusual, but gatecrashing an existing conversation or simply walking away whilst someone is mid-sentence is not ideal. I remember my first day at a new school in 2011. 'How's your missus?' Grace asked me the first time I met her. 'Er . . . she's fine,' I said. 'Do you know her?' 'No,' said Grace. She had a decent conversation opener that usually worked with most adults so Grace stuck with it. It got conversations started and then the adults managed the conversation from there on. Ross was the same. Once he knew that I support Arsenal his conversation starter would always be 'Arsenal, eh? They're not doing very well are they?' and he knew that I would laugh and then say something similar about his team, Chelsea, and then the conversation would carry on. Managing scripts for the end of conversations is important too. 'It was nice talking to you,' or 'I've got to go now. See you later,' are inoffensive and everyone then understands that the conversation is over.

Ways you can help your children with restricted and repetitive patterns of behaviours, activities or interests

Routines, rules and rituals are good ways to help take some control if the world around you is a difficult place in which to feel relaxed. In that sense schools can be good places for children with autism because they rely on routines and rules in order to function effectively, but remember that the rules are not set by the child with autism. Rules that the child may perceive to be illogical, such as keeping your blazer on and top button and tie done up when it is 30°C outside, can have the opposite effect.

No matter how rigidly organised the school, changes happen, some planned well in advance (trips, pantomimes, carol services or sporting fixtures), some at short notice (teachers covered by colleagues or supply teachers due to sickness) and some not planned at all, such as the fire alarm going off, but more likely the behaviour of another child or adult. Communicating with a child with autism and preparing them for upcoming changes is very important. How you prepare them is down to you, but the best examples I have seen are where communicating change is itself built into the daily routine. A colleague ran his morning tutor group this way, with children constructing their timetables out of laminated and velcroed squares. Mr Wilson's absence from the afternoon's English lesson would be substituted with 'Miss Blyth' or 'Supply teacher', or if the field was out of action because of the weather 'Sports Hall' was put in its place. It's not guaranteed to prevent problems arising, but you are preparing the child as best you can for known changes. You can also prepare them for some things that may not be planned. Fire evacuation drills, for example, are an obvious way to prepare a child for times when it will go off unannounced. Such times are still likely to be stressful, but the situation may be handled better than if no groundwork is done at all.

Milton et al. (2016)[10] is a very informative read on, as they provocatively put it, rules for ensuring people with autism and learning difficulties develop challenging behaviour (but they do recommend what to do about it!).

Sensory issues

Being hyper- or hypo-sensitive to information coming in from one or more of the senses can be a significant problem, not just for children with autism, but for many children with special educational needs. These sensory sensitivities can seriously affect the ability of a child to feel comfortable and to learn and can have a heavy influence on their behaviour.

It is important to recognise sensory-seeking and sensory-avoiding behaviours for what they are – an attempt by the child to have their needs met – and, more importantly, what they are not – snowflakes who just need to toughen up because it's a bit loud or because they don't want to wear the school tie. Here's a case in point:

- One of my former students, Matthew, used to eat plasterboard and Blu Tack in his mainstream secondary school. When this happened it was met with punishment, but the school unfortunately did not understand that what they were seeing was a response to heightened stress and anxiety known as pica (eating or mouthing inedible items). The punishment made the situation worse, so you can see how this became problematic for Matthew. The school could have done much to reduce his stress (caused by bullying, sadly) but did not understand, nor sought to understand, what was happening. All responsibility was placed on Matthew to change, but, of course, he was unable to cure his autism or his response to the stress that was increasing and he left there to be with us for three plasterboard and Blu Tack-free years. I wonder how they would have coped with the ingestion and smearing of faeces, which has happened in my class more than once.

Ways you can help your children with sensory issues

- Work with your special educational needs coordinator (SENCo) to create a sensory profile to help you work out how best to support your children. The Autism Education Trust's sensory assessment checklist could help here.[11]
- Accept that you will have to make adjustments for children with sensory issues. You may not like the look of ear defenders, a chewy tube (a plastic item that can be mouthed and chewed) or tracksuit bottoms instead of school trousers but these can create positive sensory experiences.
- Work out what you need to support and what you don't. A child repeatedly rocking back and forth may not be a common experience for you and you may feel the urge to stop the child doing it, but is it creating a problem that needs a solution? The child is seeking sensory input in this way and this is likely to be calming. A number of my former students repeatedly licked their fingers and then wiped them on various parts of their own body, one on the kneecaps only, and another on her cheeks, constantly during the day. The fact that it may bother you to witness it is no reason to stop it happening – it isn't disruptive to other children and they are doing it for a reason so just let them get on with it.

The National Autistic Society has some more detailed excellent advice on their website on how best to support sensory differences.[12]

REFLECTION POINTS

- In what ways do your children with autism have persistent difficulties with social communication? How can you support them to improve their social communication?

- In what ways do your children with autism have persistent difficulties with social interaction? Are there times when they prefer their own company and you should just leave them to it? How can you support them to improve their social interaction?

- Are you providing an adequate level of structure and routine for your children with autism? How do you prepare them for changes that are

---

planned well in advance? Planned at short notice? Can you prepare them better for unexpected changes such as fire alarms?

- Do your children with autism (and others) actually have sensory sensitivities? Are they over- or under-sensitive? What can you do to support their sensory-seeking or sensory-avoiding behaviours? What can you simply leave alone?

Working memory

The longer I work with children with special educational needs the more convinced I am that problems with working memory might just be the biggest common barrier facing nearly all the children I work with. It is everywhere I look. Working memory is not the same as short-term memory. If I ask you to repeat the sequence 9, 4, 8 then you are using your short-term memory, but if I ask you to say it to me backwards then you use your working memory because you have had to hold the information coming in and then do some work on it before giving your answer. Working memory is also used to hold information whilst retrieving information from long-term memory. For example, when asked the square of 16, the child needs to hold the number 16 in their working memory whilst retrieving the meaning of the mathematical operation 'squared' and the learned rules for multiplication of two numbers from long-term memory. Then they would have to hold together the products – in my daughter's case she'd currently do this by 6x6, 10x6 (twice) and finally 10x10, before adding them all together to get the answer 256. You can immediately see that if the child has never managed to securely retain the meaning of the term 'squared' or the general rules for multiplication then the task becomes impossible. Of course, eventually they may memorise, as my son who is older has, that $16^2 = 256$ by recalling it from long-term memory straightaway, reducing the load on working memory because he only has to hold 16 in there whilst retrieving the answer.

You can see that difficulties in working memory can lead to frustrations in the classroom which can result in poor behaviour or behaviours that can be regarded as poor, such as inattention or quitting tasks. It is in our best interests to recognise when working memory is a problem and do our best to help children by avoiding overloading their working memory.

The typical characteristics of working memory difficulty are:

- Appearing poorly organised.
- Inattentiveness.
- Failure to follow instructions, or forgetting part or all of a series of instructions.

- Failure to complete tasks (including quitting), or losing their place in a complicated task.
- Poor academic progress, particularly in reading and maths.

Gathercole and Alloway (2007) report that differences in working memory capacity within classes can be significant. They expect that, in a typical Year 3 class (that is to say a class of 7- to 8-year-olds) at least three children would have a working memory of an average 4-year-old and another three children would have the working memory of an average 11-year-old.[13] Consider the implications for your teaching here and what that means for differentiation.

Ways you can help your children with working memory difficulties

- Reduce the load on working memory by keeping instructions simple and expressed one at a time.
- Allow processing and thinking time.
- Reduce the amount of material.
- Use schedules (mentioned earlier in the chapter) to break down complex tasks.
- Use aide-memoires such as writing frames or multiplication grids.
- Repetition, repetition, repetition.
- Use timetables, kit lists, file dividers, dedicated pouches in rucksacks and pockets in jackets/blazers for specific items such as stationery, PE kit, money, etc. to help with personal organisation and administration.

TAKING IT FURTHER – QUESTIONS AND ACTIVITIES FOR YOU AND YOUR COLLEAGUES

- Do we have an issue in school with the over-representation of children with SEND receiving sanctions, in detention, placed in isolation and/or being excluded? If so, why is this and what are we going to do about it?

- How up-to-date are the knowledge and skills across the school on SEND topics such as autism, dyslexia, speech, language and communication needs and ADHD?

- Request practical training sessions from speech and language therapists (SALTs) or occupational therapists (OTs) (your SENCo can arrange this) or outreach teachers from your local special school on how you can support communication and sensory needs in the classroom. (Working with an OT drastically improved my teaching, by the way.) Ask them to work with you in class to model effective strategies with the children with whom you are actually working.

References

1 Department for Education (2017) Permanent and fixed period exclusions in England: 2015 to 2016. www.gov.uk/government/statistics/permanent-and-fixed-period-exclusions-in-england-2015-to-2016 (accessed 11 December 2017).

2 Ofsted (2015) School inspections and outcomes: management information. www.gov.uk/government/statistics/monthly-management-information-ofsteds-school-inspections-outcomes (accessed 11 December 2017).

3 Cohen, N.J., Barwick M.A., Horodezky, N.B., Vallance, D.D. and Im, N. (1998) 'Language, achievement, and cognitive processing in psychiatrically disturbed children with previously identified and unsuspected language impairments', *Journal of Child Psychology and Psychiatry*, 39 (6): 865–77.

4 Gregory, J. and Bryan, K. (2009) *Evaluation of the Leeds Speech and Language Therapy Service Provision within the Intensive Supervision and Surveillance Programme Provided by the Leeds Youth Offending Team*. Unpublished report. Leeds: Youth Offending Service.

5 Lindsay, G., Dockrell, J. and Strand, S. (2007) 'Longitudinal patterns of behaviour problems in children with specific speech and language difficulties: child and contextual factors', *British Journal of Educational Psychology*, 77: 811–28.

6 St Clair, M.C., Pickles, A., Durkin, K. and Conti-Ramsden, G. (2011) 'A longitudinal study of behavioral, emotional and social difficulties in individuals with a history of specific language impairment (SLI)', *Journal of Communication Disorders*, 44 (2): 186–99.

7 Van Daal, J., Verhoeven, L. and van Balkom, H. (2007) 'Behaviour problems in children with language impairment', *Journal of Child Psychology and Psychiatry*, 48 (11): 1139–47.

8 Great Ormond Street Hospital NHS Foundation Trust (2016) Information for Families: Attention Deficit Hyperactivity Disorder (ADHD). Ref 2016F1282. www.gosh.nhs.uk/medical-information/attention-deficit-hyperactivity-disorder-adhd (accessed 11 December 2017).

9 National Autistic Society (2016) What is Autism? www.autism.org.uk/about/what-is/asd.aspx (accessed 11 December 2017).

10 Milton, D., Mills, R. and Jones, S. (2016) *Ten Rules for Ensuring People with Learning Disabilities and Those Who are on the Autism Spectrum Develop 'Challenging Behaviour'… and Maybe What to Do About It*. Hove: Pavilion Publishing and Media Ltd.

11 Autism Education Trust (n.d.) National Autism Standards: Sensory Assessment Checklist. www.aettraininghubs.org.uk/wp-content/uploads/2012/05/37.2-Sensory-assessment-checklist.pdf (accessed 11 December 2017).

12 National Autistic Society (2016) Sensory Differences. www.autism.org.uk/about/behaviour/sensory-world.aspx (accessed 11 December 2017).

13 Gathercole, S. and Alloway, T. (2007) *Understanding Working Memory: A Classroom Guide*. London. Harcourt Assessment.

11

FOSTERING YOUR OWN STYLE

One has a moral duty to disobey unjust laws.

Martin Luther King

THE HEADLINES

- Behaviour is the result of interactions between people and people, and between people and their environment.

- The environment that you create for your children will have an impact on their behaviour.

- Your school's behaviour policy is a part of that environment.

- You have significant room for manoeuvre underneath that policy to create the classroom you want in order to best meet the needs of the children you teach.

- Teachers can also inadvertently misuse behaviour policies, disadvantaging certain children, including those with special educational needs.

- Bring key people such as senior leaders and those a child may usually only see for negative reasons into your classroom to see success in action.

Everything in this book has been devoted to understanding behaviour through the lens of the relationships you have with the children with whom you work. The behaviours, both yours and theirs, are the results of the complex interactions between the human beings at school and elsewhere, but are also influenced crucially by the interactions people have with their environment. This is the landscape on which your relationships are forming. How you choose to set up your classroom makes a difference. The temperature in your classroom makes a difference, as does the smell. I detested the smell of the science block when I was at secondary school, which made my choice of science teacher as a job a curious one. Where you choose to seat your children will make a difference. This is especially true for children with hearing or visual impairments who may need to sit on a specific side of the classroom or as near to the front as possible. Many of those things are within your control, or if they are not, such as the temperature, there are things you can do to help children cope with them. Headteachers look away now; I was one of those teachers who ignored our school policy that children must have their blazers on at all times unless the Headteacher announced that summer uniform rules applied. I took the view that if I felt the room was warm enough for me to remove my jacket then it was indefensible for me to expect the children to keep theirs on. I don't fall for the 'We're adults, they're children' nonsense either. Holding still-developing children to higher standards than those we expect or demand from mature, well-qualified professionals is frankly ridiculous. Secondly, and this is far more important, I trusted the children to make reasonable decisions about what they needed to do to make themselves comfortable in my class. If, by taking their blazer off, they were more relaxed and in a better frame of mind to pay attention and to learn without being disruptive to others then it seemed petty of me to deny them the chance to do this. I didn't view blazer removal as an act of defiance or the precursor to a student insurrection. This need to control everything because, if we make a concession by allowing a child to take their blazer off, chaos will ensue smacks of insecurity. It reminds me of General Melchett, the parody First World War army officer from *Blackadder Goes Forth* when he says, 'Give 'em an inch and before you know it they've got a foot. Much more than that and you don't have a leg to stand on.'

A major part of the environment within which you, your colleagues and the children are working is your school's behaviour policy. It is obviously designed to help you do your job, although rarely we may have all come across policies that seem to do precisely the opposite. A good whole-school behaviour policy provides the basis for consistent practice amongst the adults in the school and offers support when you need it. You can lean on it when you're out of ideas and it can be the comfort blanket you need when you're new to teaching or when you've just started at a new school.

However, it can also get in your way. Whole-school policies can mandate practices you may want to reject or that you fundamentally disagree with. You may feel that your school's policy is overly restrictive or, worse, too lax; that it adds to your workload or that it doesn't involve you in the process enough.

How do you go about fostering your own style from within the boundaries of a school's behaviour policy? People like me get bent out of shape if colleagues aren't consistent, but this is not the same as being mindless or robotic. Some things in a policy are non-negotiable, but there should always be plenty of room for you and your personality and your principles to shine through. I did, however, leave a school early on in my teaching life when I felt the system was overly restrictive, both for me and for the children stuck in the middle of it. I was told by my boss soon after starting at the school that he preferred it if the children worked in silence with the work put up on the board, and that practical work was better done individually and in silence. That was enough for me to decide that I should work elsewhere.

I strongly encourage you to ask questions of the senior leaders in your school about the behaviour policy you are expected to support. Good leaders will welcome this and will be happy to explain why policies have been set up in a certain way. It would be concerning if they can't explain to you, or if they are defensive about their policies. As the science writer Jacob Bronowski[1] says, 'Ask an impertinent question and you are on your way to a pertinent answer.' You may well have good suggestions as to how behaviour policies can be improved and I encourage you to put these to your senior leaders. Your experience at the chalkface is valuable and good leaders will recognise this.

You make the weather in your classroom, as the saying goes (well, apart from PE teachers), so it is inevitable that the relationships developed between the human beings in your classroom play a large part in how heavily you lean on the school's behaviour policy. Your sense of humour, how you create the learning environment, your passion for the subjects you are teaching, the humanity of your responses to stress, crisis, struggle and conflict, the encouragement you give to students when they feel helpless, the interest you take in their lives, the fact you give a damn and go the extra mile by making the effort to contact home when things have gone well all accumulate into your identity as a teacher.

REFLECTION POINT

- Take a fresh look at your school's behaviour policy. What does it actually insist upon? What is advisory? Identify areas where you can decide for yourself how you want things to be in your classroom.

Setting children up to fail

Fostering your own style can sometimes feel a little like subverting the system. Despite demands for consistency from people like me, situations will always play out differently in every classroom. You can find your own space in the system in good ways, but you can also subvert the system in ways that are bad.

In my first school the behaviour policy was based on a warning system. It was designed to provide children with a number of chances to modify their behaviour before they would be removed from the classroom by a member of the senior management team. Each warning came with an associated sanction and these escalated in response to non-cooperation. This was behaviourism once more. The first warning carried with it a success reminder; the second resulted in losing a small amount of time; the third a faculty detention; the fourth resulted in an after-school detention; and the fifth meant that the child was removed from the lesson and remained in isolation for the next lesson you had with that child (which could be a fortnight away). Five warnings is of course too much, but the design almost guaranteed escalation, especially as warnings were often given publicly and sometimes with a flourish. In the early days with some classes I had many names up on the board with tally marks against their names to keep track and this was the most obvious indicator to any visitor that I had lost control of my lesson. I could have done this on a piece of paper, but had stupidly decided that the public display would communicate to the children the seriousness of what was happening. Of course, it had the opposite effect – the children amassing warnings found it amusing and others whose learning was being disrupted would become exasperated by this indicator of my lack of control. You could see it around the school too. I would walk into a lab after someone else's lesson or walk around the school and see tens of warnings on whiteboards – those were lessons on life support. Worse was to come, though. I started putting certain children on two or three warnings before the lesson started. I even wrote them up on the board before they walked in. I know, I know, what was I thinking? The honest answer is that I wasn't thinking at all. I had kidded myself that I was being tough and sending a firm message to the child, 'Look, this is serious now. You've got fewer chances so sort yourself out. I'm helping you and being kind by doing this to you.' In reality the ink was already dry on the exit ticket. I didn't invent this; I was advised to do it by one of the school's behaviour experts. I take all the responsibility for being an idiot and shamefully writing those children off, but it shows you how little we even discussed such egregious subversion of our own system in our school. This was unacceptable subversion and I'm ashamed that I ever did it. It must be so damaging for a child to walk into a classroom knowing that the dice are loaded against them from the start. These were precisely the group of children that needed more support from me, and I ham-fistedly robbed them of it.

REFLECTION POINT

- Are there aspects of your school's behaviour policy that make it harder for certain children to be successful? How can you mitigate against that?

I've been on the receiving end too. In the same school we had a lottery ticket system for rewards. We could award children lottery tickets when we felt they went over and above. I remember as a PGCE student awarding George, who was regularly in trouble for poor behaviour, a lottery ticket in a chemistry lesson for weeks and weeks of fine effort. At the end of every term all the tickets were put into a big drum and a number of them drawn out in assembly, leading to prizes. I was told before the assembly that George's ticket, along with a host of others, had been taken out of the pile, as 'we can't have certain kids winning prizes in front of the whole school'. I was furious, but lacked the courage to take a stand on it. My professional judgement had been dismissed, but worse, George's efforts had been airbrushed out of history. Children in these systems don't stand a chance if teachers like me set them up to fail with warnings they haven't even earned and, to compound the problem, their well-earned achievements are then erased in an Orwellian 'Oceania had always been at war with Eastasia' style.

Haim Ginott's hard-hitting words from the start of Chapter 3 need to be re-emphasised here, especially where he ends with – 'In all situations, it is my response that decides whether a crisis will be escalated or de-escalated and a child humanized or dehumanized.' You can use a school's behaviour policy as a lever to get rid of a child or you can make sure that it works to your advantage and that of the child as you reach out a hand to help them up each and every time they need you.

REFLECTION POINT

- Are there aspects of your school's rewards and recognition policy that are effectively out-of-bounds to certain children? What can you do to mitigate against that?

Perpetually positive

Behaviour policies exist to cope with times when behaviour is less than good. As a result they tend to focus predominantly on responses to poor behaviour. They are also likely to contain information on the school's reward system, but in essence they are negative, responsive documents. They are far less likely to mandate what you must do in order to provide a positive and uplifting environment for your classes, which is where your own personal style comes in. They are also unlikely to get anywhere near the fine details, the day-to-day interactions that underpin superb behaviour in classes. This is the space you can flood with your own on-the-field tactics of positivity so that your class has that buzzy, purposeful feel that can't be faked or generated by a climate of fear. Some may be more prescriptive. A friend of mine is the Headteacher of a school where he insists that all classes have an alphabetic boy/girl seating plan. Personally, this is too far for me as it gives no thought as to how those pairings may or may not work. I'm also fairly sure that gender imbalance and other factors make this impossible, at least part of the time. He has his reasons and I respect them, but I still fundamentally disagree with them. That element of agency is not available to the teachers in that school, but much still is in play for them to decide what to do in their classes.

Maybe your school has those effort sticker charts for each class that I mentioned in Chapter 5 – I know many primary schools that do. Who says it has to be on public display? If you feel the need to award effort stickers, and you're sure that effort is what you are really recognising, then stick the chart in the stationery cupboard out of sight. Why are you even keeping score? Does it really matter? You could just as easily make a note in your markbook and put the chart in the bin.

The same goes for traffic light behaviour systems. I advised you in an earlier chapter to bin your traffic light system, but if your school insists you have one on display then keep the important bit, the bit where you advise the child how to improve their behaviour, and ditch the public part where you move their name to the amber or red lights for all to see. Just leave them all on green. It'll soon become redundant through lack of use, and then you can accidently on purpose cover part of it with some other display.

Your school may not yet use restorative principles to resolve conflict. There is nothing to stop you using them in times such as detentions or on the playground or in the corridor. For sure, a whole-school approach is likely to be far more effective in the long-term, but you can pioneer such practices by getting the training you need in order to learn how to do it properly and then share successes with colleagues.

REFLECTION POINT

- Are there any behaviourist customs in your school that you can simply cease doing?

Despite some of my early mistakes that I shared above, I also had some successes. One of my most successful tactics was to spread the word about children who were making good progress in improving their behaviour.

I was fed up with us as a school having a downer on particular children like George mentioned above. It is one thing to sit in the staffroom and talk about how well George is getting on, but this can stray dangerously close to 'Well, I never have any problems with him in my class!' Instead I decided to try a different tack. I would approach the form tutor, the Head of Year, the Deputy Headteacher responsible for behaviour and the Headteacher and ask them to drop into my lesson for two minutes to see a particular child. I would brief them by letting them know how things had been going and ask them to take a walk around, show interest in everyone, of course, but make sure they looked through a particular child's book and make a fuss of them by telling them that they'd heard how well they'd been getting on in physics. It wasn't always possible, but it had a lovely impact on the child when they knew that good news about them was spreading. I also wanted the managers to see up close that this child was succeeding somewhere, as they were more likely to come across them for negative reasons. The child also then had a positive interaction with an adult that they more often than not associated with negative situations. I can reinforce here once more the power of sending good news home. Again, your school is unlikely to mandate this, but you can go to town on this tactic. Spreading good news far and wide is always an easy win. It does, however, come with one health warning. I've tried to take this tactic of spreading good news to assemblies with mixed success; it has backfired on more than one occasion. This is because some children hate very public recognition or being centre of attention and I hadn't given enough thought as to how they might react to such exposure. I had one teenager sob uncontrollably in assembly once when I tried this. On another occasion a child who had made massive strides in his behaviour won an academic award and I tried to present it to him in assembly only for him to refuse to come up. You all know that I should have read the signs and left it there, but instead I walked up to him in his seat and handed him the certificate. I walked back, still with the certificate in my hand and a two-fingered salute for my trouble.

REFLECTION POINT

- How can you spread the good news about progress with behaviour though your school? Who needs to come in to see it in action?

Those mistakes that I made in my early days happened primarily because I relied too heavily on the school's behaviour policy. I had yet to fine tune my classroom practice well enough and had yet to develop my professional confidence to a sufficient level. I remember clearly that I really started to feel like I was motoring in my fifth year of teaching, but I still didn't think deeply enough about behaviour; I didn't discuss behaviour with my colleagues in any depth; I didn't read anything by Bill Rogers or Rob Long, for example. I learned the hard way, which I guess almost all teachers do with behaviour, but it also took me far too long to learn and to become competent. I still recall the first ever whole lesson I taught when I was training. I was teaching Year 9 to make loudspeakers and, as trainee teachers are prone to do, had spent about three hours planning a one hour lesson. Within 40 minutes I had dried up. Everything I had on my lesson plan had been done and I was as helpless as a newborn. The Deputy Headteacher whose class it was, was at the back observing. I simply looked at him and mouthed 'HELP'. He stood up, strolled to the front and cracked on seamlessly from where I'd beached myself. I had an empty toolbox whereas he had a pedagogical Swiss Army knife seemingly ready to cope with any situation. It's the same with behaviour. In the early days you can be floored by situations that are brand new to you, but the sooner you start to develop an inner assurance and confidence that you can deal with much of what schools can throw at you the sooner that translates into a feeling of security and safety for the children in your care.

Don't rely on your school's behaviour policy to do the heavy lifting for you. It is there to support you, so please don't assume that I suggest you ignore it, but it doesn't substitute the human and humane touch that you bring. Be bold and set out your classroom the way it works best for the children who are learning there. Be perpetually positive, be restorative, be proactive and you will find that you have to lean on the school's policy less and less.

TAKING IT FURTHER – QUESTIONS AND ACTIVITIES FOR YOU AND YOUR COLLEAGUES

- How prescriptive is our behaviour policy?
- Are there things in there that we insist upon that we could reasonably leave to individual teachers to decide how to implement in their own classrooms?
- Could we make protected time in staff meetings for teachers and support staff to share what's working behaviour-wise in their classes?
- Have I got used to using behaviourist strategies such as behaviour traffic lights that I could stop using with immediate effect?
- What do I need to substitute them with, if anything?

Reference

1   Bronowski, J. (1973) The *Ascent of Man*. London: BBC Books.

A FINAL WORD

Our job is to teach the students we have. Not the ones we would like to have. Not the ones we used to have. Those we have right now. All of them.

Dr Kevin Maxwell

Trying to figure out how to improve behaviour can feel like looking for a golf ball in a snowstorm. You can be wandering around with your arms outstretched, trying to lay a finger on this elusive goal whilst squinting through the blizzard searching for the tiniest of signs that you are on the right track. The footprints you can see in the snow might be yours from a path you made earlier or they might have been laid down by any one of a multitude of other teachers who are all searching in solitude for the same thing. Unfortunately there are no neon signposts to point you definitively in the right direction, and there are no snow ploughs clearing an easy and direct route to your destination.

There are, though, team-mates and allies in the form of parents, teaching assistants and fellow teachers who can all support each other to make it more likely that you will all achieve the goal for which you are all striving.

There are opportunities for you to jettison along the way the redundant equipment that is weighing you down, such as faulty thinking or the use of ineffective punishments. There are chances for you to replace that old kit with newer, more effective equipment, such as restorative practices, that will help you pick up your pace and maintain momentum.

There are morale boosters at your disposal, such as unconditional positive regard and your emotional investment in the child, which mean you will keep going when things get tough. These will help you to challenge those who predict failure and you will see this as a nervousness and a professional insecurity that is the communication of their unmet need to feel safe and secure.

There are waypoints you will recognise along the way, such as an increase in intrinsic motivation of a child that will reassure you that long-lasting behaviour change is within reach.

I hope that this book has provided you with much to think about, helped you reflect on the great work that you are already doing and given you a leg-up to make things even better. I'd be delighted to hear how you get on. Thanks for spending this time with me.

Jarlath

SELECT BIBLIOGRAPHY

Biesta, G.J.J. (2015) *Beautiful Risk of Education*. Abingdon: Routledge.

Blair, C. and Raver, C.C. (2015) 'School readiness and self-regulation: a developmental psychobiological approach', *Annual Review of Psychology*, 66: 711–31.

Blair, C. and Razza, P.P. (2007) 'Relating effortful control, executive function, and false belief understanding to emerging math and literacy ability in kindergarten', *Child Development*, 78 (2): 647–63.

Burchinal, M.R., Peisner-Feinberg, E.S., Bryant, D.M. and Clifford, R.M. (2000) 'Children's social and cognitive development and child care quality: testing for differential associations related to poverty, gender, or ethnicity', *Applied Developmental Science*, 4 (3): 149–65.

Cross, M. (2011) *Children with Social, Emotional and Behavioural Difficulties and Communication Problems: There Is Always a Reason*. London: Jessica Kingsley.

Dix, P. (2017) *When the Adults Change, Everything Changes: Seismic Shifts in School Behaviour*. Bancyfelin: Crown House Publishing.

Dreikurs, R., Cassel, P. and Dreikurs Ferguson, E. (2004) *Discipline Without Tears*. Etobicoke, Ontario: Wiley.

Driver, R., Squires, A., Rushworth, P. and Wood-Robinson, V. (1994) *Making Sense of Secondary Science: Research into Children's Ideas*. Abingdon: Routledge.

Kohn, A. (1993) *Punished by Rewards: The Trouble with Gold Stars, Incentive Plans, As, Praise and Other Bribes*. New York: Houghton Mifflin.

Kohn, A. (1996) *Beyond Discipline: From Compliance to Community*. Alexandria, VA: Association for Supervision and Curriculum Development.

Milton, D., Mills, R. and Jones, S. (2016) *Ten rules for Ensuring People with Learning Disabilities and Those Who are on the Autism Spectrum Develop 'Challenging Behaviour'... and Maybe What to do About it*. Hove: Pavilion Publishing and Media Ltd.

Mitchell, D. (2014) *What Really Works in Special and Inclusive Education*. Abingdon: Routledge.

Muijs, D. and Reynolds, D. (2011) *Effective Teaching: Evidence and Practice*, 3rd edn. Los Angeles, CA: Sage.

Myatt, M. (2016) *High Challenge, Low Threat: How the Best Leaders Find the Balance*. Woodbridge: John Catt Educational.

O'Brien, T. (2015) *Inner Story: Understand your Mind. Change Your World*. CreateSpace.

Rogers, B. (2002) *Classroom Behaviour: A Practical Guide to Effective Teaching, Behaviour Management and Colleague Support.* London: Paul Chapman Publishing.

Vanier, J. (2008) *Becoming Human.* Mahwah, NJ: Paulist Press.

Webster, R., Russell, A. and Blatchford, P. (2016) *Maximising the Impact of Teaching Assistants: Guidance for School Leaders and Teachers.* Abingdon: Routledge.

INDEX